PLANNING A WEDDING

The Essential Guide

Laura Gartside

Planning a Wedding – The Essential Guide is also available in accessible formats for people with any degree of visual impairment. The large print edition and eBook (with accessibility features enabled) are available from Need2Know. Please let us know if there are any special features you require and we will do our best to accommodate your needs.

First published in Great Britain in 2012 by
Need2Know
Remus House
Coltsfoot Drive
Peterborough
PE2 9BF
Telephone 01733 898103
Fax 01733 313524
www.need2knowbooks.co.uk

Contents

Introduction

Congratulations! Deciding to get married can be one of the most exciting and wonderful moments in a person's life, and it will hopefully be followed by many more as you and your partner spend your lives together. Of course, planning a wedding can seem a complicated or even daunting affair, but it doesn't have to be that way. With the help of this book and just a little bit of forethought you will find that an awful lot of stress and hassle can be avoided, leaving you in control and free to enjoy your big day with your friends and family.

The book is divided into 11 chapters, and it covers the main things you will need to think about as you prepare for your wedding. It assumes a 'Master Timeline' of 9 months from announcing your engagement to ceremony, and includes a handy 'Countdown Checklist' which includes a fine breakdown of everything talked about in the book. Of course, the style and size of your celebration will affect the number of things you need to think about and, naturally, it is wise to allow yourself more time the bigger the party it is going to be. However, irrespective of the number of guests you intend to have and the time constraints you may be facing (and even if you're thinking of hiring a wedding planner to take some of the organisational strain), you will find lots of helpful information in this book, including:

- How to allocate your budget, and stick to it.
- Top tips for researching and negotiating on goods and services.
- Must-know legal essentials.
- What to look for in an entertainer.

Also, it is important to consider what pitfalls to avoid when making decisions about your wedding day. With the sheer amount of information that you will be faced with when weighing up your options, it is very easy to be misled from your original plans or take things for granted. So whilst it is a common mistake (and a very easy one to make) to assume, for example, that your cake supplier shares your exact vision, or that your venue will automatically provide table linen at no extra charge, it can be a difficult trap to climb out of without additional costs and ill-feeling. This is why, at the end of the book, you will find checklists of questions to ask a supplier before writing a cheque. You can photocopy these and put them in your wedding folder to easily compare venues and food suppliers, and to help ensure you get the same information from all of them.

It is also worth asking yourself if you have thought in enough detail about the role of your friends and family on the day. Weddings are rich with traditions and full of pre-prescribed roles for many people, but families and social circles now have the potential to be incredibly divergent, and may not fit the traditional model. Equally, the couple getting married or entering into a civil partnership have far more freedom to dictate the order of the day and the level of formality required, but it is worth remembering that your loved ones may have their own preconceived ideas about how your wedding should be. Have you thought if this applies to you? If so, have you thought about how to solve the problem without hurting anyone's feelings or sacrificing your own dreams? This is where chapter 8 – Etiquette and Expectation Management will be particularly useful. It covers everything from modern approaches to the gift list and speeches, right through to strategies for heading off or minimising familial conflict. It may not seem like an easy thing to tackle, but remember: you're not alone! There are lots of fantastic ways that you can ensure everyone has a wonderful, relaxed time at your wedding, and this chapter will leave you brimming with confidence that you can successfully navigate any tricky conversations that may lie ahead.

Throughout the book I have also included alternative ideas for the contemporary wedding, which cover everything from bouquets and banquets to veils and vows. Nowadays, many couples are choosing to personalise their day in ways that are unconventional but deeply meaningful to them, and this can also be a wonderful way to save money whilst leaving your guests with unique memories. So whether you want to express yourselves with quirky table decorations, handcrafted stationary or even go as far as one couple I know and hand sew your own 14th century wedding robes . . . the sky's the limit!

Most of all, this book will help you concentrate on the most important thing: you and your future spouse. It is imperative that you both have memories you can cherish for many years to come, and the single best way of leaving yourself free to do that is to ensure the logistics of everything are organised in advance. All you have to do is follow the advice in this book, and you'll find that your big day is everything you could have wanted. So let's get planning!

Chapter One

Initial Preparation

Setting a budget

The cost of getting married varies hugely. Although there are some essentials that must be paid for, (see chapter 4 – Legalities and Paperwork for further details), ultimately the amount you spend on your wedding is dictated by your circumstances and the preferences of you and your partner. Be warned though – it can be very easy to become swept up in the idea of a perfect fairy-tale wedding, and there is seemingly no limit to the number of bridal magazines and websites telling you about 'must-have' products and concepts. Inevitably, this can make the costs of the day spiral out of control, which is why it is important to determine how much you are going to spend at the outset and stick to it. You can help yourself do this in three ways:

Involve your partner

The chances are that one of you will be more excited about planning your wedding than the other. This is fine and perfectly normal, but it is a day for both of you, and it is likely that your future spouse will have at least one or two ideas about how they'd like things to be. Tackle this carefully though, and remember that you're only looking for broad ideas – now is not the time to be asking about seat cover sashes. Instead, try asking things like:

- Would they prefer to keep it a fairly low-key and intimate affair, or if they would like a huge celebration with as many friends as possible?

- When should you get married? Do you need to consider holidays, children, illness, tours of duty, international guests, pregnancy, work commitments etc.?

How do they expect the wedding to be paid for? It may sound silly and like a question you should already know the answer to, but it is essential to check this with your partner now. It would be very unfortunate to get any further in the budgeting with one or both of you assuming, for example, that money will be arriving from the other one's family when it will not. Be upfront with each other now about if any financial support will be forthcoming from your parents and how much you will be able to save from work between now and then.

Prioritise

Now that you know roughly when your wedding will be, how big you would like it to be and an idea of how much you can put towards it, it's time to choose what is most important to both of you. Sit down and brainstorm all the things that really matter. Do you have your heart set on one magical venue or a particular dress designer? An award-winning photographer a must-have? Is it crucial that you throw the best party your guests will ever remember? Or is it something simpler like a particular person conducting your ceremony, or your vows containing a particular reading or quote? Write everything you really want down whether it has a material cost or not, and then start to rank them. If you have lots of very detailed ideas, force yourself to choose just five as this will really help you focus on what is important to you.

Remember: It's great if your partner wants to be involved in this too, but if they don't, just keep this list of priorities safe, and refer to them whenever you need to. Feel free to change them further down the line, but *always* limit yourself to five 'essentials' at any given time. If you manage this, any compromises on items that didn't make your list will seem like less of a loss and you'll be surprised at how much easier it is to stick within your budget!

Set an error margin

Once you know what you can afford to spend on your wedding, divide the number by 10. Then multiply this number by 9. This is what you should actually aim to spend on your wedding, and will leave you with a 10% error margin for unexpected costs. For example, let's assume you can raise £12,000 for the cost of your wedding.

- £12,000 ÷ 10 = £1,200.
- £1,200 x 9 = £10,800
- £10,800 is your final budget

It may seem tempting to avoid this step, but in the long run it is really not worth it. Don't think of it as doubting your ability to stay in within budget, but rather proof of your foresight and capability.

Place, time and people

You will also need to consider when and where you will have your wedding, and (if the decisions might impact each other) who you really want to be there. This isn't just about choosing the exact times and venue, but also the broader geographical location, and approximate time of day. Consider the following points to help you decide on the when and where.

Place

- Non-local and international guests – People travelling from far away will need somewhere to stay, and possibly good transport links. Is the place you are considering reasonably accessible? If not, should you consider subsidising travel expenses? Be aware that travel costs are potentially a huge issue, and may be a deciding factor for some people.

- Guests with mobility issues – Do you have any guests who are elderly, frail or wheelchair users? Do they need any special assistance getting to and/or moving around your location? If so, how are you going to support them?

Time

- Guests with children – unless you specifically veto it, (which can be a very unpopular move), the larger your guest list, the more likely you are to have children at the wedding. If they are very young they may not last very well for a whole day's worth of celebrations, so consider having a 'drop out' point after the main meal so families can celebrate with you without worrying if they will appear rude for leaving halfway through.

Top tip:

Try writing all your ideas down on a new line of the paper, and cut them out so you can physically move them around in a hierarchy.

- Day – What day of the week do you want to get married on? Saturday is often the most popular day for a wedding and tends to book out a long way in advance, but often venue rates are cheaper from Monday to Friday. Think about your guests again. Are most of them likely to be 9-5 workers? If not, it may be worth considering a weekday.

Top tip:

Try to avoid going to wedding fairs before you are prepared with questions, and never, ever allow yourself to be pressured into making a commitment on the spot. A good supplier will always be committed to helping you make the choice that's right for you.

People

- Who do you want as bridesmaids and ushers?
- Which other guests are essential?

Preparing to negotiate

How to research

Now that you have settled on a location and ideal time, you can think about approaching venues. To begin with, find out about as many options as you can in the area you've chosen. Search the Internet, ask friends, and make use of the many wedding forums available online (see the help list at the back of the book). The chances are that there will be people there who have got married or are planning a wedding in your area, and they may be able to recommend (or warn against!) certain suppliers and venues. Request wedding brochures and packages from any venues that offer them, (hotels, conference centres and stately homes nearly always have these), and for hotels in particular it is a good idea to ask if they have any wedding fairs coming up soon.

Conversational gambits

It may sound odd, but it's really worth paying attention to your language when approaching suppliers. It's absolutely normal to feel intimidated by this, particularly when discussing large sums of money, but the right approach can pay dividends and really get people 'on your side'. And remember – these are the people who you will be relying on to ensure your day is everything you have dreamed of. The golden rules of opening negotiations are as follows:

- Smile! Be relaxed, and remember that you have every right to ask questions, and then walk away to reflect on your options.

- Ensure you are speaking to a decision maker – a simple 'Hi! I'm interested in the options you can offer me for my bridesmaids' dresses, decorations, banquet – who can I speak to about that please?' will do it. If you get a way into a conversation and realise you are not speaking to someone who has the authority or knowledge you need, don't be put off. Smile again, and say, 'Gosh, I'd really like to get this sorted today though – who else is here who could help us?'

- Presume the positive. Say, 'Can you be flexible with the price?' instead of, 'I don't suppose you can offer a discount, can you?' Or, 'Can you adapt that colour for us?' instead of, 'Doesn't it come in any other colour options?' It is human nature to want to answer in the affirmative, and everyone wants to be seen to be flexible and willing to adapt.

- Be sensitive to your supplier's situation. This is particularly important if you are dealing with, for example, a family firm of artisan cake makers or professional musicians. They have skills that have taken years to acquire, and there is a limit to how much you can (and should) ask them to discount their service. On the day, good feeling and a willingness to ensure you are happy is far more important than a last £10 off the price.

- Take details, and say you hope to follow up. Always, always, always walk away, even if you both feel it's a great deal. If you agree to buy multiple cakes (for example) on the assumption you'll just cancel all the ones you decide against, you will be in a very awkward position if something happens to your first choice.

- Watch for the 'tiara trick'. So named for the moment when the bride sees herself in 'The Dress' for the first time, and the sales assistant pops a tiara on her head to finish the look. It's a perfect moment and the temptation is not to care about another £80 on top of a dress that costs £1,000. But you should. You've already done so well negotiating up until this point, so don't be thrown off by a sales technique. (Besides, if it really is the perfect tiara it will still be the perfect tiara after you have gone away and looked at others in your own time!) And remember, last-minute upselling is not limited to dresses. The 'complimentary glass of champagne we can give your guests on arrival for just another x' or the 'exclusive use of the room for the whole day' are not things to make on-the-spot decisions about. They may sound like comparatively small sums of money, but together they can really add up.

To tell or not to tell?

An often repeated piece of advice to brides-to-be is not to tell suppliers that they are actually getting married. The theory is that if you tell a hairdresser you want your hair styling for a school reunion or family get-together, he or she will not automatically double the price. This is absolutely your decision, but I would personally advise against it for several reasons:

- In the case of hairdressers and make-up artists or similar, you are relying on them to make you look good in photographs you will hopefully have forever. Ensuring they know this may well provide an incentive to work extra hard with you prior to the event, and be absolutely clear about what you want. Moreover, hair and make-up trials are often sold as part of the service, so effectively you are asking professionals to do their work twice. It is therefore reasonable to expect to pay more than usual.

- For any 'on the day' services your suppliers will work out pretty quickly that this is not a school reunion or Uncle Albert's 80th, and this will lead at the very least to bad feeling. In a worst case scenario, you may be confronted with a demand for extra fees or threat of no service.

- Remember, you can (and should!) always ask outright about pricing structures. Ask what the price for a regular room hire/meal for 100 people/ photography session is, and then ask about wedding prices. Assuming there is a difference, ask the supplier to explain it. You may be pleasantly surprised and decide there are indeed good reasons why photographers and caterers charge more for a wedding, or you may not. If you are not happy with the justification, move on and try someone else. You are the one in control!

Wedding planners

As you are reading this book, you obviously want to manage your own wedding. However, in addition to a complete orchestration of the event, did you know that wedding planners can be asked to oversee just parts of your day? This can be everything from ensuring RSVPs have returned, to acting as master of ceremonies, or just ensuring guests know how to move between venues. Naturally, they also have terrific industry knowledge and can negotiate substantial discounts on products. But if you do decide to delegate a small amount of your wedding planning, remember to ask the following things to any wedding planner you approach:

- Can you provide references?
- Can you demonstrate that we will save more than your fee on our wedding costs?
- Are you a member of any overseeing body?
- What do you offer as a guarantee?

In the UK, wedding planners are not legally obligated to hold any particular certification or registration, but members of The Wedding Association (www. weddingassociation.co.uk) are required to produce recent references, evidence of training and evidence of trading for over three years.

Make a wedding organiser

Well done! Now that you've made the key decisions, it's time to start the really fun side of wedding planning. You'll be collecting lots and lots of information though, so the best thing to do is ensure you have a place to keep it all. Of course, you can buy one of the many pre-made wedding organisers available, but these are expensive, and creating your own allows you to tailor it entirely to your own needs.

If you have access to spread-sheet software (e.g. Microsoft Excel or the free OpenOffice Calc), arranging the information in a workbook can be helpful, but it is also perfectly possible to do it with pen and paper. Personally, I recommend using both; Excel will allow you to easily create a running total of expenditure, but physical writing is much more convenient when taking notes during a conversation with a supplier. Therefore, to make your wedding organiser you will need the following items:

- A ring binder.
- Dividers.
- Photocopies of the following from this book:
- The questions to ask each supplier (at the end of the relevant chapter).

- The master checklist.
- Supplier Contacts Page.
- Guest list spread-sheet.
- Plastic wallets to hold smaller literature such as flyers and business cards.
- Guest list (do not worry if this acquires many alterations and crossings out over time!).

Summing Up

- Involve your partner.
- Set and stick to your five priorities.
- Think about location in terms of the most important guests.
- Prepare questions and practise your best smile for negotiating.
- Make your wedding organiser.

Chapter Two

Traditions

Weddings have many traditions attached to them, but it is not always clearly understood why. This is a shame as many of those concerning the ceremony itself are rich with symbolism, and can be a wonderful way of incorporating your culture or beliefs that you find attractive. Similarly then, having an understanding of the traditional roles of the wedding party can help you to ensure that as many people as possible are included in this most important of events. It also helps to ensure that no one person is overburdened with responsibilities!

Allocation of duties

As will be discussed at the end of the book, it is by no means compulsory to assign any given task to a specific person. However, it is still a smart move to know the traditional roles fulfilled by the wedding party as it helps to ensure nothing is forgotten about. As a bonus, you can also refer back to it when saying 'but it's traditional' suits your purposes!

Familiarise yourself with the list of wedding duties below, organised by the person who traditionally takes the responsibility. At the back of the book you'll see all of these tasks again with space to fill in your own party's names. This will provide you with a clear record of exactly who is responsible for what, and thus the peace of mind that nothing is forgotten and no one overburdened.

Bride and groom

- Welcoming guests to the reception.
- Cutting of the cake.
- Commencing the first dance.

Groom

Second speech, after the father of the bride's

Best man

- Organising the stag night.
- Ensuring the groom gets to the ceremony on time.
- Keeping the rings safe until they are passed to the groom/given to the ring bearer.
- Third speech, after the groom's.
- Reading out messages of goodwill from absent friends.
- Ensuring the wedding presents are stored safely.

Chief bridesmaid/maid of honour/matron of honour

- Helping the bride dress.
- Travelling with the bride to the ceremony.
- Organises all other bridesmaids, page boys and flower girls.
- Managing the bride's train as she walks down the aisle and stands in front of the celebrant.
- Holding the bride's bouquet during the vows.
- Making the fourth and final speech, the 'Reply to the Best Man'.
- Ensuring the wedding presents are displayed nicely.

Groomsmen/ushers

- Greeting and directing guests to their seats as they arrive.
- Distributing Order of Services.
- Escorting the bride's and groom's mothers to their seats.

- Marshalling people for the group photographs.
- Encouraging mingling amongst guests by initiating introductions.

Bridesmaids

- Assisting the bride in organising the wedding party dress.
- Assisting the bride in wrapping the table favours.
- Travelling with the bride to the ceremony.
- Standing by her as she takes her vows.
- Encouraging mingling amongst guests by initiating introductions.

Flower girl

- Walking ahead of the bride up the aisle scattering petals or confetti etc.

Page boy

- Acts as ring bearer.
- Walks with the flower girl in the recessional.

Toastmaster

- Announces the entrance of the bride and groom to the reception.
- Announces each speech.
- Announces the cutting of the cake.
- Announces the first dance.
- Introduces the entertainment.

Who pays?

Historically, the bride's family have taken all of the financial burden. However, over time this has changed, and it is still considered traditional if some of the expenses are to be met by the groom's family and the newly-wed couple themselves. A more realistic breakdown of who pays for what may look a little like this:

The bride's father

- Engagement announcement.
- Wedding planner.
- Wedding insurance.
- Hire of the reception venue.
- Catering at the reception.
- Save the dates, invitations and postage.
- Clothes and accessories for the bride, bridesmaids, flower girl and page boy.
- Transport for the bride and himself, bridesmaids and the bride's mother to the ceremony venue.
- Flowers to decorate the ceremony and reception venue.
- Photographer.
- Wedding cake.
- Accommodation for close family that have travelled a long way.

The groom's parents

- The parents' meeting following the engagement announcement.
- Their own outfits.
- Wedding present for the newly-weds.

The bride

- Hen party.
- Groom's ring.
- Present for the groom.

The groom

- The stag party.
- Bride's wedding ring.
- His and his ushers' suits.
- Transport for the best man and himself to ceremony venue.
- Ceremony fees.
- Presents for the bride and bridal party.
- Transport away from the reception venue for himself and his new wife.
- Bouquets and button holes.
- Wedding night venue.
- Honeymoon.
- Press announcement for wedding.

The bride and groom

- Present for the bride's and groom's parents.

Of course, many couples now marry later in life and are already successful professionals who are not financially dependent on their family. They may also not be marrying for the first time. Even if neither of these apply, a couple may just not feel comfortable asking the bride's family to bear the brunt of the cost, and that is before considering how much control you may be asked to relinquish in exchange for monetary support! This can be a tricky area to navigate, but below is a list of options that could help you negotiate the issue of money successfully:

- Start saving. Unless you are very fortunate, you will almost definitely need to make a contribution yourself. It may mean cutting out a few luxuries for a while, or scheduling in regular overtime, but the sooner you start this the better. Make sure that it is maintainable until the date of your wedding, and give yourself a fixed target such as 'I will put aside £100 per month towards the wedding'. Then make sure you put this into a separate account – ideally a savings account. Then leave the account card at home!

- Volunteer your projected expenses to the families. This completely transparent approach may work if you think your families would like the opportunity to pay for specific items, but it will leave you open to criticism, resentment and embarrassment from all sides about your choices. A better option is to state the total budget, and ask if they would like to make a contribution.

- Be fair. If you know that you and your future spouse earn more than your parents, consider whether or not you have a moral obligation to meet all of the costs. However . . .

- Be sensitive. Even if you have been married before and your family made a significant contribution to that wedding, your parents may still have a clear sense of 'duty' to pay. If this applies to you, balance your realism with protecting their pride. This is another good reason for slightly 'fudging' the total cost of the day (in a downwards direction) if need be!

- Consider alternative sources of income. You may wish to consider a loan, but considering the majority of weddings in the UK cost between £5,000-£15,000 this should be approached with caution, and you must be certain of your ability to pay it off.

One of the biggest problems that can occur, however, is when one family is considerably better off than the other but does not want to foot the entire bill. In this scenario the best thing to do is accept whatever they are willing to give, but under no circumstances discuss the other family's contribution.

Need2Know

Where do some of the wedding traditions come from?

Something old . . .

To help you enrich your wedding with symbolism, why not take a look through the list of traditions detailed below? Some, like the wedding ring, will almost certainly already be part of your plans, and you may wish to incorporate others that you find particularly attractive. However, even when there is nothing you wish to amend, you may find that knowing the origin of your intended actions adds an extra layer of meaning to the moment. You could even request that the significance of a ritual or element is explained to your guests, either by the celebrant or in the speeches afterwards. It's a wonderful way to personalise your day and can create a real sense of emotional involvement for everyone present.

Rings

The ring has been part of the wedding ceremony since antiquity, and has appeared in many different forms as fashions and beliefs have changed. It is commonly thought to have first appeared in ancient Egypt, where plaited reeds were made into rings or bracelets and exchanged at marriage. As now, the circle was seen as a symbol of eternity, but the hole was also significant, representing the gateway into married life. It is also from Egypt that the ancient Greeks adopted the idea that the left finger contained a vein – the 'vena amoris' – running directly to the heart.

However, the practice of wearing a plain gold wedding ring was a comparatively late idea. The Romans initially preferred iron as a symbol of a man's strength and protection, and in medieval Europe stones such as rubies and garnet were sometimes set into wedding rings, as they were considered to be symbols of love. In Renaissance Italy, silver became the metal of choice for both betrothal and wedding rings, and throughout Europe rings are also sometimes worn on the right hand. This is usually a cultural tradition, with people from Eastern Europe being more likely to wear a wedding ring on the third finger of the right hand.

Confetti

Confetti, which literally means 'sweets' in Italian, is often thrown over the newly-weds as they exit the ceremony. In the UK, flower petals, seeds and, later, rice were used, as it was believed they promoted fertility. In Mexico, red beads are also sometimes used.

The white dress

Wearing white on one's wedding day is, of course, synonymous with the bride's purity. However, given that this has been a crucially important quality in a future wife across many civilisations it is a surprisingly modern adaptation. It was first made popular in 1840 when Queen Victoria married Prince Albert, and eschewed the silver dress traditionally worn by royal brides.

Bridesmaids

Although it is now considered poor manners for anyone but the bride to wear white, cream or ivory at a wedding, this has not always been the case. It is thought that the original purpose of bridesmaids was to protect the bride from evil spirits, and one way in which they did this was by wearing similar dresses to the bride. This would apparently confuse any malevolent presence, and it would depart.

Veils

Veils are also rich in meaning, and in Roman times would serve a similar purpose to the bridesmaids. They would also have been bright red or gold to mimic fire, which was thought to be the best defence against any nasty supernatural elements that may try to intervene at the ceremony. Of course, there is also widespread thought that veils stem from the less romantic practice of preventing a man from seeing what he had agreed to marry before it was 'too late'! This idea is partly reflected in Jewish ceremonies, where a groom will lift the bride's veil and study her face for a moment to ensure it actually is his intended before the beginning of the ceremony.

Shoes on the car

In Tudor times, guests threw old shoes at the departing newly-weds, and if one hit it was considered good luck for the couple and the thrower. This has now been replaced by the practice of dragging old shoes on strings behind the vehicle that takes the bride and groom away from the ceremony.

The cake

Although the wedding cake in its current form is an invention of the 20th century, a cake in some form has been traditional at weddings for centuries. However, the significance around the cake has changed. The modern practice of cutting the cake together is said to symbolise embarking on a joint partnership, and the feeding each other a metaphor for looking after and providing for one another. However, previously a bride may have cut the cake alone as a symbol of the impending loss of virginity, and even earlier, the wedding cake would have been broken over her bride's head to promote fertility. However, if this is one ancient tradition you wish to resurrect, it may be worth waiting until the photographs are finished!

5 almonds as favours

Sugared almonds are the traditional wedding favour as they are intended to represent the bittersweet nature of married life. Traditionally five are given to represent health, wealth, happiness, fertility and longevity.

Shared wine glass

This was originally a French tradition, where each family would bring a bottle of wine to the reception, and pour a little of each into one glass. The bride and groom then both drink from this glass, symbolising the permanent mingling of their families, and their binding to each other. Other modern 'unity ceremonies' that are popular are the mixing of coloured sand in a jar, and the simultaneous lighting of one large candle with two smaller ones held by the bride and groom.

Groom standing on the bride's right

Rather gallantly, it is thought that the groom stands with the bride on his left so that his (right) sword arm is free and he can defend any last minute attempts to kidnap her!

Carrying the bride over the threshold

The practice of carrying the bride over the threshold is also thought to stem from a traditional UK belief that it will protect the bride from any evil spirits that may be hiding in the doorframe.

When to get married

An old English superstition is that weddings should commence when the minute hand is ascending, as this is when it is pointing to Heaven. In addition, May is often said to be an unlucky month for weddings, and it is even rumoured that Queen Victoria banned her children from marrying in May! However, June is considered lucky, possibly because it is named after Juno, the Roman goddess of love and fertility.

Sixpence in the shoe

This is still done by some brides in the UK to encourage wealth in the marriage, although these days a penny is usually substituted as sixpences are difficult to come by.

Thirteen gold coins

In many Hispanic cultures, the groom makes a gift of thirteen gold coins – 'las arras' or 'unity coins' – to his new bride during the ceremony. These are often presented in an ornate pouch or container to the priest by a designated person in the wedding party, who blesses them. The priest then gives the coins to the groom, who pours them into his bride's hands as a symbol of his trust in her and a promise to provide for her financially.

First purchase

A common folktale in the British Isles is that the person to make the first purchase after marriage will have the upper hand in the relationship. It is therefore traditional for the bride to arrange to purchase a pin off her chief bridesmaid immediately after the ceremony.

Celtic traditions

All countries have wedding customs that are particular to their history, but it is the Celtic traditions that gave rise to some of the most romantic and enigmatic practices in the British Isles. The following rituals are believed to have originated in Scotland, Ireland or Wales, and many are still practised today.

Creeling

This is a Scottish practice which uses the creeling pots normally used in lobster fishing. The pot is filled with heavy stones and tied to the groom's back, who must then chase his bride around until she agrees to kiss him.

The engraved silver spoon and carved wooden spoon

These are given to the bride by her husband as a gift upon marriage as a symbol of his love and intention to provide. The silver spoon is given in Scotland, whilst the wooden spoon is given in Wales, and is traditionally hand carved by the groom.

Feet washing

In Scotland, a bride-to-be will have her feet washed by her friends, including at least one happily married woman. The married woman also drops her wedding ring into the water before the washing commences to bring good luck, and it is believed that the girl who finds the ring will be the next to marry.

Bridal kidnapping

Particularly in Wales, there has long been an elaborate and theatrical practice of people attempting to 'kidnap' the bride. Traditionally, this begins on the morning of the wedding with the groom trying to force his way into the bride's house against her family's will, only to eventually run around it and not recognise her due to her being disguised. The bride's family may also seize her from the door of the chapel and drive off with the groom in pursuit, and even after the wedding the bride can still be chased! Originally she would have been pursued on horseback by the groom and his ushers, on the premise that one year from that day she will love the man who catches her.

Wearing/carrying of horseshoes

Horseshoes are now a well-recognised symbol of luck the world over, but they have long been of particular significance to Irish brides, who carried them on their wedding day. This is still done, and the horseshoe must always be upright, so that the luck doesn't fall out.

Salt and oatmeal

In both Scottish and Irish weddings, the bride and groom may wish to eat three spoons each of salt and oatmeal before the ceremony starts, as this is thought to ward against the evil eye.

Summing Up

- Traditional roles and responsibilities should be seen as a helpful guideline rather than rules.

- Exploring traditional wedding practices can be a wonderful way to represent your cultural heritage on your big day.

- Be sensitive and realistic about the financial implications of your wedding.

Chapter Three

Venues

There are certain questions that need to be asked of any venue that is involved in your wedding. Some – 'will this fit the number of people I want to invite?' – are quite obvious, but some others, such as the acoustic properties of a given room are less so. However, don't despair! By making sure you follow the list of pointers following, you can be certain that every last detail is thought of, and that your final choice of venue will be exactly what you need.

For all venues

Take your wedding planning checklist and a camera to each venue you visit. It will really help you remember exactly how things look afterwards, so during your visit you can concentrate on the following questions:

- What dates do you have free in the month we are considering? (Remember that Sundays through to Thursdays are often cheaper than Fridays and Saturdays.)

- Have you had a wedding ceremony/reception in here before?

- What deposit do you need, when do I need to pay the balance by and do you offer an instalment plan?

- What are your recommended and maximum capacities? (If possible ask to see photographs of the venue set up for a similar event.)

- How accessible is the venue for guests with mobility issues?

- What decorations, if any, are included in the room rental price?

- Do you have someone onsite who can liaise directly with my florist/caterer etc.?

- In the event of a fire or other emergency, will someone who knows the building be on hand to assist with evacuation?
- Do you have a hearing aid loop system? If necessary, can you provide microphones/sound systems, and is there and extra charge for this?

Top tip:

Ask if you can see the venue at roughly the same time as you would like to hold your ceremony, as this will give you the best idea of how it will actually look on the day. Always check everywhere your guests may go, including both bathrooms and designated smoking areas.

Ceremony venues

Certain questions only pertain to the ceremony venue. When considering your options, make sure you mentally walk through the event as it would happen. Where would your guests congregate whilst waiting for you both? Do either of you require getting changed onsite, and if so are there facilities for this? And of course, check that the venue is actually licensed to be a wedding venue.

Confetti and photograph protocol

At the venue where the actual ceremony will be held, it is always wise to check in advance if there is any restriction on confetti. Some places, such as municipal buildings, may have a complete ban. Others may request that confetti is only thrown in a particular area, and still others may request that only biodegradable confetti (or rice) is used. Similarly, some historic buildings restrict photography in certain rooms, or ban it completely during the ceremony itself. Many ceremony venues will state their stance on both upfront, but in case they don't – just ask!

Choosing a celebrant

At the heart of any wedding day is the ceremony itself. Undoubtedly the most important part of the day, the importance of choosing the right person to conduct your ceremony cannot be overstated. It is therefore vital that you spend some time thinking about what you will require from the ceremony itself, as this will impact on who can officiate at your wedding and therefore the venue for the ceremony. (See chapter 5 – Legalities and Paperwork for more information).

Reception venues

As with places to hold your ceremony, reception venues have their own list of things to consider. Chiefly, these are to do with feeding and entertaining your guests, although you will also need to consider how your guests (and you!) are going to travel from ceremony to reception venue if not on the same site. Ensure you are prepared by having clear ideas about the following:

Seating plans and escort boards

If you are having a seating plan, (which we discuss further in chapter 8 – Etiquette and Expectation Management) you will also need to consider where the escort table or board (which lists your guests' names and the seats they are allocated to) will be located. You can buy, hire or even make yours, but check first if your venue can already provide one – it can save a lot of money!

Decorations

In addition to asking what decoration a venue provides, consider how your preferred colour scheme will work in context. Traditional floral centrepieces are expensive at the best of times, so don't waste money on anything that might look jarring. Similarly, if your venue has particularly ornate furnishings such as wall or ceiling murals, consider leaving these as the feature and removing details such as chair sashes and centrepieces: It will prevent an overly fussy look and save money into the bargain. Alternatively, if you want something completely different and cost-effective there are lots of creative options for table decorations, including:

- Origami (flowers or other shapes).
- Jars or bottles filled with sweets, pebbles, sand, strings of lights etc.
- Arrangements involving dried/artificial blooms, seashells or feathers.
- Candles.
- Personal items from the couple's home.
- Trivia about the couple or weddings in general.

Top tip:

Ask about alternative access points to the venue in the event of roadworks.

Centrepieces don't even have to be particularly formal or elegant – one of the most fun weddings I ever went to had a different game from the couple's childhood on each table. The unexpected opportunity to play things like Buckaroo, Hungry Hippos and Operation generated a lot of interest and amusement, and served as a fantastic ice-breaker. It also meant that guests were highly motivated to walk around after the meal to see what else they could play, and strike up conversations with each other.

Duration and aftermath

Always check with your reception venue how long you can have the space for, and if there are any 'overstay' charges. This may be less of an issue in a hotel, for example, but in buildings that do not regularly clean up after large numbers of people there may well be a surcharge. Also make sure that you and the vendor mean the same thing by 'clearing up'. Even with loyal family and friends to assist, there is nothing worse than spending your wedding night trying to pick up the pieces from a huge party when you should be enjoying your first night as a married couple!

All-in-one packages

It may be that you would like to avoid the hassle of moving guests between venues, and if so an 'all-in-one' package deal may be the best option for you. This is the most commonly found option in hotels, although increasingly other venues that are licensed to hold a ceremony are opening themselves up to the party afterwards. There certainly are definite advantages and disadvantages to this type of wedding, but with the right information you can be certain of making an informed choice.

Pros

- An all-in-one venue is likely to have a dedicated wedding co-ordinator onsite who will be familiar with the building and oversee the complete smooth running of your day.
- It is very likely to have experience in organising weddings.

Top tip:

As with all aspects of your wedding, make sure that you realistically cost any home-made alternatives you choose, and build in more time than you think you will need to actually get them made.

Need2Know

- Additional finishing touches, such as a cake stand and knife are often included in the price.

- Menus and drinks packages are constructed with the minimum of fuss.

- Local services, such as DJs and florists can nearly always be recommended, and sometimes discounts offered if booked through the venue.

- Prices are usually stated per head, and a clear, fixed list of what is included in the price is stated upfront.

- Serving staff are nearly always provided and well trained.

- If the venue is a hotel, discount room prices are usually offered to guests for overnight stays.

Cons

- Food and alcohol prices are likely to be at a premium.

- There can be very little flexibility with menus offered, and you may have to provide the same meal for all your guests.

- Opportunity to decorate to one's own theme can be extremely limited.

Outside spaces

It may well be that you have the option to do something really different on your big day, like getting married in the formal gardens of a stately home or a zoo. Getting close to nature can, of course, provide a wonderfully romantic backdrop for your nuptials, but it does come with its own special checklist of things to watch out for:

Ensuring bad weather alternatives

If you are having any part of your ceremony outside, the first thing you will need to consider is a bad weather alternative, and how quickly a change can be made. For example:

Top tip:

Remember that even set package prices do not always include VAT, and this can make a significant difference to your final spend.

- Is the bad weather alternative close enough that in the worst case scenario – a sudden and torrential storm mid-ceremony – guests can be moved swiftly and with the minimum of disruption?
- If you would prefer to remain outside but employ an overhead covering, will it be sturdy enough to survive an onslaught of bad weather?
- Do you wish your canopy to be erected from the start of the ceremony or can it be quickly raised? Who will be responsible for this?

Many outside venues offer an inside alternative as part of their quoted price, but always make sure that this is the case.

Acoustics

Acoustics in open air spaces can be terrifically difficult to predict. They can be impacted by the size of the open space, the amount of wind on the day and, of course, the size of your wedding party. Ask what audio options are available and permissible to ensure that no one misses out on hearing the all-important 'I do'!

Members of the public

A final thing to consider if choosing an outside venue is members of the general public. If you are planning to marry at a tourist attraction it is extremely unlikely you will be able to secure the venue only for you and your guests, and the proximity of strangers may be less than ideal.

Transport

We have already touched on transport as an important factor to consider in your wedding when moving guests between venues, but there are other things to think about as well.

For the couple

Traditionally, the groom makes his own way to the church or registry office and a bride is driven there separately. However, there are now a great number of situations where this may not be seen as a practical arrangement (e.g. the couple intend to dress in the house they already share on the morning), not a relevant arrangement (e.g. there are two grooms or two brides), or just not what the couple getting married would like to do. The important thing to remember is that you and your future husband or wife should feel comfortable with whatever is decided. In both cases, here are the key points that you should factor into your decision-making.

Sticking with tradition

If the bride's arrival will be a feature of the proceedings, many options are available to you. Classic cars and horse-drawn carriages are always popular, but there are an increasing number of companies willing to provide other, considerably more unusual options. You may wish to arrive in something that reflects the location of your ceremony, any theme you might have, or you and your partner's profession. Within the UK it is certainly possible to hire emergency service vehicles, (internally converted for comfort or left in original condition), rickshaws, sedan chairs, tractors, JCBs, 'toy' trains (of the type that have an engine and wheels, and often transport children round zoos, theme parks etc.), helicopters, boats or even a hearse for the ultimate gothic wedding! However, if you and/or your partner are making an entrance, remember to ask yourself the following questions in each circumstance:

- Is this transport available on the day that I need it?

- Is the driver licensed and insured?

- Will I be able to safely fit into it and walk from it on arrival?

- Will it alter what to tell my photographer, or what I need from them?

- Does my or my partner's arrival clash with instructions I would otherwise have given the photographer?

- Is this vehicle legally allowed and physically able to cover the route from where I will be picked up to the wedding venue?

- For items such as helicopters and hot air balloons, what permissions need to be granted in regards to landing, who is responsible for this, what will it cost and when are the deadlines?
- Will the weather affect the transport or your appearance if there is wind and rain?

www.weddingsday.co.uk list many wedding transport companies across the UK, and are a fantastic place to start looking for both traditional and alternative options. However, if none of this sounds particularly appealing, that's fine too. Asking a friend or family member to drive you to the ceremony is a truly lovely way to let people help out, and certainly a comparatively cost-efficient one!

Alternatives

Particularly if you and your future husband or wife live together, you may wish to dress and travel together. It may be seen as unromantic by some, but many couples like the reassurance of having their fiancé(e) present on the morning of the ceremony. Even for the best prepared amongst us this can be a very stressful time, and you may later be grateful to have your best friend around. It will also give you both some precious time together at the start of the day, which will definitely be in short supply once the actual festivities get underway!

As always, talk to your partner and be honest with yourselves and each other about what you really want. If your heart is set on a grand entrance you now have the tools to organise it smoothly, but if you would prefer something more low-key you should also feel comfortable asking for it.

For the guests

Whether or not you provide transport for the guests at any stage will depend on a number of things, not least of which are your budget and the distance which they have already travelled to be with you on your special day. For example, do you want to organise cabs or a minibus between ceremony and reception venues, or would it be acceptable to let people find their own way there by foot or on public transport? Would people be happy to car share? These are all perfectly acceptable options but do remember that if left to make their own arrangements, guests *will* take much longer to move to the

Top tip:

In preparation of guests leaving after drinking, have the numbers of four or five local cab firms that you trust. It won't seem excessive if suddenly there is a mass exodus of people all wanting to be picked up.

next place you want them to be, and this will in turn impact your schedule for the rest of day. It's also possible, if they are in a strange town, they will simply become totally lost! However, if your budget just doesn't run to transport for the entire party, you can appoint locally based 'marshals' on the day to get people moving in the right direction and furnish guests with hand-drawn maps.

Summing Up

- Always visit the venues you are interested in.

- Take photographs so you can compare venues side by side in your own time.

- Get all offers in writing.

- Venues often need to be booked well in advance – make the decision about both as soon as possible to secure your ideal time.

Chapter Four

Food and Drink

After setting the date for your wedding, one of the first things you will need to organise is the catering. This includes the main meal, cake, beverages, possibly a drinks or canapé reception and finishing touches such as edible favours. The food is likely to be one of the things most guests remember about your wedding, but by following these simple guidelines you can ensure that everyone leaves with full stomachs and big smiles on their faces!

The main meal

The chances are that you will want to provide your guests with at least one main meal after your ceremony. You may choose a traditional sit down meal or 'wedding breakfast', a hot or cold buffet, or something a little bit more unusual. You may even choose to enlist friends and family members in the preparation of any food you serve, but each of these options has its own special considerations, as outlined below.

Seated meal

This is the option that is most likely to be offered to you if you are planning your reception in a hotel, civic building or tourist attraction. Normally, venues that specialise in weddings will have an in-house catering team who will offer wedding packages with staggered pricing structures, and/or a 'menu selector'. These can be a very convenient and low fuss way of doing things, but you will almost always be asked to choose the same meal for all of your guests, and many brides find this awkward. However, if you are happy with this then make sure that all of your guests' needs (see overleaf) have been thought of.

Alternatively, if you are having the reception in a venue that will allow you to bring an outside caterer in, you have a far greater chance of negotiating a choice for your guests. Realistic expectations are key here though: you may have to tell your caterer well ahead of time what people have chosen, (inserting a menu selector into your invites is an excellent way to manage this), and it is unlikely that anywhere will be able to offer more than three or four options per course.

Hot and cold buffets

Buffets can be an absolutely fantastic idea for food at a wedding, whether they are the main or only meal, or if they are brought out later on while the evening entertainment happens. It is also easy to include lots and lots of variety. However, you should always ask if the company provide their own tables, crockery and linen, or if this is something that would be your responsibility. You should also ask about the staff that will arrive and unpack it. Normally you will pay an hourly rate for individuals to unpack, wait on the tables and clear away the debris at a certain point, so make sure you are clear about how much you are being charged for what with all your suppliers.

Guests with special requirements

The larger your party is, the greater the chances are that you will have guests with special dietary requirements. Broadly speaking, these will fall under the subcategories of:

- Allergies and other medical requirements (e.g. coeliac disease, Crohn's disease, lactose intolerance).

- Cultural and religious requirements (e.g. halal, kosher).

- Lifestyle (e.g. vegetarianism, veganism).

Naturally, you will want to accommodate all of your guests' requirements where possible, and even if you think you are familiar with their needs, double check for fine details to watch out for! For example, there are many different levels of kosher observance, vegetarians cannot eat gelatine or cheeses that contain rennet and most vegans abstain from honey.

Doing it yourself

If your wedding is smaller and less formal, (and you have helpful and willing family and friends) you could consider providing a home-cooked wedding breakfast. This is a wonderful way to involve loved ones and will allow you to know exactly what you are serving, but it is potentially hazardous. Think seriously about how much time it would take in advance and on the day, and who would be kept away from the party and for how long. On the other hand, barbeques and hog roasts in a back garden allow guests to mingle and chat around and in front of the food, and a picnic can be prepared largely in advance. Just remember to ask yourself the following questions:

▨ Do I/my friends and family have the skills and resources to prepare, cook and serve food to a wedding party of this size?

▨ How will I provide options for people with special requirements?

▨ Where will I source it from and how far in advance should I order?

▨ Where will the food be stored and eaten?

▨ If it is in a public space, (e.g. park or beach) do I need any special permission to take a large group of people there? Do I mind if the general public are present?

▨ Do I have enough crockery and cutlery?

Timing considerations

It is also very possible that you will want to provide a second meal during the dancing and entertainment. The good news is you can make this a much simpler affair as most people will probably still be full from the wedding breakfast and cake. You should also ensure that it is not something that will require people to be sat down to enjoy – this is the part of the day where you want guests to be moving around and enjoying themselves, so finger food that can be picked at is ideal.

Top tip:

It is often convenient to ask guests to note dietary requirements on their invite RSVPs, but a few informal enquiries beforehand also helps!

Questions for the main caterers

Here is the essential checklist of questions to ask potential caterers. Depending on your circumstances some may not apply, but most will:

- Are you free on the day required?

- Have you provided catering at my venue before?

- What staff will you provide to set up, serve and clean up the food?

- How much choice are you willing to offer my guests, and what notice of menu choices do you require?

- What experience do you have in catering for guests with special requirements?

- Is your menu customisable? Can you give us a quote for a meal including a particular dish?

- Do you provide any decoration for buffet tables?

- What do you offer for children's meals and what are they priced at?

Champagne and canapé receptions

When and where is it necessary?

Even at the best planned wedding, there will be periods of time when your guests are hanging around. Depending on how you have structured your wedding this may be as they are arriving and waiting to go into the ceremony or during the photographs. Providing your guests with something to drink and/ or nibble at as they mingle is a good idea, but don't be tempted to over-order and risk ruining people's appetites or having a large amount of waste. Also, think realistically about how much time people will have to consume anything you have provided. Photographs will normally take far longer than waiting for all your guests to arrive, for example, so in the latter instance you may wish to just provide drinks.

How to prioritise and choose options

- Be realistic about how long this 'holding period' will last, and how much food – if any – you will need. A good rule of thumb is 1 canapé per guest per 10 minutes, or 1 per 15 minutes if going straight on to a meal.

- If your budget is limited, consider a prosecco or other sparkling wine instead of champagne.

- Always ensure that water and soft drink options are available.

Beverages

Alcohol with food

Most couples will want to offer their guests alcohol with the main meal, but even if you are avoiding this for religious, cultural or personal reasons stick to the portions outlined below with your substitutes. It can seem impossible to anticipate how much people will want to drink, but an average of ½ a bottle of wine per person plus champagne or sparkling wine for the toasts is very reasonable.

It is also advisable to have a straight 50/50 split between red and white wine. Even if you normally have very defined ideas about matching particular wines with particular foods, it is worth remembering that your guests may not, and will definitely appreciate being given a choice. If you are not wishing to serve alcohol, you could consider providing flavoured mineral water, fruit juices or non-alcoholic wines etc. Whatever you decide, make sure there are at least two options available.

Top tip:

To make the wine go further, ask the waiting staff to walk around the tables topping up glasses rather than leaving the bottles on the tables for guests to help themselves.

Cash bars

A cash bar is a facility at your wedding where your guests will be able to purchase their own drinks. Usually this is provided by the hosting venue, as specific licences have to be held in the UK to sell alcohol at private functions. Hotels and restaurants will nearly always be willing to offer this, and some other venues are willing to organise temporary cash bar licences. If setting up a temporary licence, venues will require a certain degree of notice (see the master timeline) but it is a great way to ensure your guests have access to a much broader selection of drinks at no extra cost to you. They can also be used as the sole source of alcohol if you do not wish to purchase or consume alcohol yourself, but would like to give your guests the option to do so.

Top tip:

Top tip:

Many package venues such as hotels will initially state that corkage is just not an option with them, but don't be put off! If they understand this is potentially a deal-breaking decision they may well make an exception for you.

Toast options

Depending on the number of speeches, you may find yourself being required to toast several times. Traditionally, speeches occur after the main meal has been served, although, increasingly, couples are choosing to have them prior to the meal to get them out of the way. As with a 'champagne' reception, you do always have the option of choosing a far more cost-effective sparkling wine, which can save a significant amount of money. Alternatively, if you would prefer to stick with the real thing then you do not necessarily have to buy the most expensive variety available. Champagne is a luxury item and the sort of thing that everyone loves to splash out on – particularly on such an important occasion – but it is highly unlikely that your guests will be able to taste the difference between one type and another.

Corkage and sale or return

Sadly, it is not uncommon for venues to charge a premium on wine to go with food, as you and your guests are very much a captive audience. However, there are always alternatives! For example, it is nearly always cheaper to buy your beverages from a specialist wine merchant on a 'sale-or-return' basis, which simply means that you will be able to return any unopened bottles after the big day is over and get your money back. Even if you have chosen to have a wedding breakfast package, it is always worth asking if there is an option to be charged a small amount of 'corkage' to open and serve alcohol you yourself have provided. To work out how much corkage you need to ask for, subtract the cost of the sale-or-return wine from the cost of the venue wine. Any corkage charge agreed with your venue must be lower than this figure.

Lastly, if you are sourcing your own drinks, make sure to clarify the following well in advance of your wedding:

- The terms and conditions of your preferred wine merchant.

- When the venue will need the drinks delivered by.

- How they will be stored.

- Who will be responsible for serving them.

- When the venue will require unopened bottles to be uplifted?

The cake (and alternatives)

This classic option is still much taken up my many couples, but it is by no means the only route. Some other avenues that you may wish to explore are:

- Different types of cake (e.g. chocolate, victoria sponge, cheesecake).

- Healthy options.

- Revisiting childhood (jelly cakes, candy tables, cupcakes, candyfloss).

- Tower puddings (e.g. croquembouche).

- Savoury alternatives (tiered wheels of cheese, pork pies, towers of sushi).

The Internet is a great place to start looking for inspiration, and don't be daunted by all the options! All you need to choose is something that you and your partner will enjoy eating. Also, for brides on a budget, (and depending on the complexity of what you choose), this part of the wedding can also be one of the easier options to do yourself, or enlist a friend or family member to take control of.

However, if you are purchasing your cake (or alternative), be sure to ask the following questions:

- Do you offer complimentary tasting?

- Can we see a previous portfolio of wedding cakes, in similar designs, if at all possible?

- Do you offer transport and professional set-up at the venue?

- Do you include loan of cake stand, knife and toppers, and if not what is the charge?

Top tip:

If you require something elaborate, choose a cake designer that specialises in wedding cakes. Not only will you be more likely to see a portfolio including designs similar to the one you want, but they will have the special training to meet your expectations.

- What happens if the cake is damaged in transit or whilst on display?
- When does the cake booking need to be finalised and paid for?
- What are the cancellation deadlines and penalties?
- What if I'm just not happy with the cake?

A reputable cake maker will want to give the best possible cake, but it is also helpful to take some of your ideas along. For example, if you want any part of the cake decoration to coincide with your stationery/bridesmaids' dresses/flowers etc., try and take along a fabric sample or bloom. Also take pictures with you from bridal magazines or printed from the Internet of cakes that you find attractive. If possible, ask for literature to take away with pricings and options.

Edible favours

Many couples still choose to give edible favours at weddings, although the choice now is far greater than the traditional offering of sugared almonds. Of course, you may prefer to present your guests with one of the hundreds of options of non-consumable favours (if you are giving them at all), but if you'd like to offer a little sweet treat there are particular things to think about:

- How do the favours need to be stored before transport on the day?
- Will they be okay to be left at room temperature for a morning whilst the reception venue is set up?
- How far in advance do I need to order or start making them?
- Do I need to buy from a supplier who produces in a nut-free factory?
- Do any of my guests need a diabetic version of the sweets, and is this obtainable?

In addition to this you could also consider offering sweets with a local connection, such as miniature Kendal mint cakes, Cornish fudge, Irish brandy balls or Scottish tablet. Alternatively, you could recreate your childhood with traditional penny sweets in pick 'n' mix bags. Or why not have your favours personalised? There is literally no limit to your options.

Summing Up

■ Be sensitive to your guests' dietary requirements.

■ Always taste the food before agreeing to a contract.

■ Offer guests a choice of beverage.

■ Don't order too many canapés and hors d'oeuvres.

■ Use a specialist wedding cake maker if possible.

Chapter Five

Legalities and Paperwork

Essentials of getting married

Fundamentally, marriage is a legal contract, and as such demands certain requirements of the parties entering into it. These vary slightly depending on whereabouts in the UK you live and where you wish to marry, but broadly they are the same. However, extra care should be taken if you have very unusual circumstances, such as one party being housebound, hospitalised or detained. For the most comprehensive advice available check your local authority's homepage and also the Citizen's Advice Bureau.

Who can get married?

In the UK, two types of ceremonies leading to marriage are recognised: religious ceremonies and civil ceremonies. In addition to this, same-sex couples are able to enter into civil partnership, which gives the couple the same legal protection and rights as mixed gender couples. There are very slight technical differences between all three, (see overleaf), but generally the rules for marrying or entering into a marriage or a civil partnership are as follows:

- In England, Wales and Northern Ireland, both parties must be 18 or over on the day of the wedding, or 16 and over with parental consent. In Scotland, persons over 16 can marry.

- Neither party can be currently married or in a civil partnership.

Top tip:

It is highly advisable to ensure the registrar has the notice four weeks before the proposed date, or six weeks if one or both of you has been married before. It may seem overly cautious, but it is absolutely worth taking just a little extra time to ensure that nothing will trip you up when there is no time to sort it out!

- The individuals wishing to marry cannot be closely related. (The list of excluded relationships is listed at www.adviceguide.org.uk if in doubt. Be sure to check under the part of the UK you are resident in!)
- Both parties must be consenting to the marriage and capable of understanding the ceremony.
- In Scotland, the marriage would have to be also regarded as valid in the country/ies to which either party belong.

Note

Although the difference is mainly one of semantics, in the eyes of the law, same-sex couples *only* have the option of entering into a civil partnership and mixed sex couples *only* have the opportunity of entering into a marriage. However, if you are in a same-sex relationship and would like a religious ceremony, why not approach your faith leader and discuss if they can help make your beliefs a part of your day? It never hurts to ask!

How to get married

Civil ceremonies

If you wish to have a civil ceremony, the good news is that you are free to marry in any approved location. However, you will need to register your intention to marry in your local register office. The superintendent registrar (or registrar in Northern Ireland) will then issue authority for the marriage.

In England and Wales, both partners must be resident in England or Wales for seven days before notice is given. A notice must state where the marriage is to take place. The marriage can then take place after 15 days have elapsed from the date on which notice of the marriage is entered in the marriage notice book, and this is also the same in Scotland.

Religious ceremonies

In some circumstances in the Church of England and Wales, (and where the person conducting your ceremony is also authorised to register the marriage) you may be able to avoid visiting the superintendent registrar. Instead, you can have notice of your intention to marry read out on three occasions prior to the wedding. (This is called 'the banns'). However, check well in advance with the person conducting your ceremony if they are qualified to do this. If they are not, you will need to visit the superintendent registrar.

In both cases, you and your partner will be asked for certain documents when registering your intention to marry. Generally, this will include the following:

- Proof of name and address.

- Proof of date of birth.

- If one partner has been married before or in a civil partnership, documentary evidence that the marriage or civil partnership has ended. Most commonly this would be a decree absolute or a death certificate. These can take time to obtain, so make sure you build them into your timeline.

- Proof of nationality.

A variety of documents can be used as evidence of the information required, but you should always contact the registrar (or the religious representative if they are authorised to register your marriage) concerned for the most up-to-date information. They will be able to provide you with comprehensive details of what is necessary.

When you have registered your intention to marry, you will be issued with a marriage schedule. This is a vitally important document as it must be presented to the person conducting the ceremony on the day, and no marriage can take place without it. Furthermore, it will need to be collected by either the prospective bride or groom – so make sure that any well-meaning relatives aren't sent on a wasted journey for you!

Who can conduct a marriage or civil partnership?

Top tip:

Although children under 18 cannot be a legal witness, it is not unknown for a registrar to allow a teenager to sign in the book if two adult witnesses have already done so. This can be a lovely way to involve a younger person, but do be aware it is entirely a goodwill gesture on the part of the registrar and not something you can or should insist on.

Civil ceremonies

Civil ceremonies must be conducted by a superintendent or deputy registrar in England and Wales. In Scotland there is also the option to have a legally binding civil ceremony conducted by a humanist celebrant.

Religious ceremonies

If you wish to have a religious ceremony, then you must be married by a priest, pastor or similar officiant within your religion. However, this person must have a certificate or licence to conduct weddings from the local superintendent registrar. If they do not, a registrar must attend the religious ceremony. If this is not possible a separate civil ceremony must be held for the wedding to be legal.

Vows

Whether you marry in a religious or civil ceremony, you will be required to make certain promises in front of the registrar. (This may be the person conducting the ceremony, or they may simply be present to hear them, depending on your circumstances.) Whilst the legally binding vows cannot be changed, they can be added to; although it is worth noting that in a civil ceremony nothing added can be overtly religious.

Witnesses

Whether you marry in a religious or civil ceremony, you will need to make your vows and sign the register in front of at least two people. These individuals are your witnesses, and can be absolutely anyone. You can have up to four witnesses sign in the register for you, and the only requirement for witnesses is that they are over 18 and have been present through the ceremony.

Costs of each stage

Charges vary dependant on your local authority, and are always subject to change. Furthermore, the cost for an attending registrar at an approved location is set by your local authority, and places of worship may also have their own fees. However, the below prices are a good guideline.

- Giving notice to marry (each)   £30-£33.50
- Civil wedding or civil partnership   £40-£55
  at registry office
- Copies of marriage certificate   £3.50

Name changing

Although by no means a legal requirement, many couples choose to take one partner's surname or combine them into a new double-barrelled surname. However, the list of the potential forms to fill in and number of people to contact can seem quite staggering at first! Added to this are uncertainties about procedure and seemingly impossible conundrums such as travelling abroad mere hours after your name has changed, and amending one's surname can quickly seem like an intimidating task. However, in this section we will be looking at some of the essential things to consider if you or your partner are changing your surname. It should not be viewed as exhaustive, but together with the master checklist (which has space to add your own people to contact) it will certainly put you on the right path!

How many copies of the marriage certificate?

It is always a good idea to purchase an extra copy of the marriage certificate for the purposes of changing records afterwards. This is because many organisations such as the DVLA, your bank and the passport service will want to see the original. Therefore, if the worst happens and your marriage certificate goes missing in the post, you will have a spare on hand, and even if it doesn't you will still have one at home to photocopy for anyone who is satisfied to see a duplicate. Marriage certificates can also be requested later on through www.direct.gov.uk. [Government, citizens and Rights, Registering Life Events, Birth, Marriage and Death Certificates.] As of 2012 the fees are £9.25 for a standard service and £23.40 for a priority service.

Passports

If you are lucky enough to be honeymooning abroad, you will of course need your passport to travel. If you will not be changing you name however, then you do not need to alter your passport. However, if you are intending to change your name then you will need to inform the passport and identity service. The question is; when, and how?

The first thing to do is contact the travel company and/or holiday provider and ask if they need the name on your passport to match the name that any tickets are booked in. Also check with any airlines you may be travelling with. Many will not let you travel under a passport with a new name, even if you are carrying your marriage certificate. However, it is often recommended that you wait to change your passport until after you have returned from your trip, as even if your travel company is willing to let you board, the country you are travelling to may not let you enter their borders.

If you are 100% certain you are not constrained by this, you do have the option of applying for a name-amended passport on the grounds of marriage up to three months before the ceremony. Your old passport will be cancelled and the new one sent to you, but it will be post-dated to the day of your name change, so you will not be able to use your passport for travel or as legal ID until then. To apply for an amended passport go to the DirectGov website and download the relevant form.

Household documentation

Your household documents will also need to be updated with your new details. On the opposite page there is a handy checklist of people you may need to contact to tick off, as well as some space to write down and tick off anything that occurs to you!

Banks .... ☐

Mortgage provider/Landlord .... ☐

Credit cards.. ☐

Passport Service .... ☐

DVLA... ☐

Pension provider .... ☐

European Health Travel Insurance (Previously E111) .... ☐

Insurance companies (home, contents, car, health, life etc.) .... ☐

Local authority for council tax purposes .... ☐

Electoral roll.. ☐

Utilities, i.e. gas, electricity, water and sewage.............. ☐

Internet, landline and cable/satellite provider .... ☐

Trade union.. ☐

Mobile phone companies .... ☐

Doctor... ☐

Dentist .... ☐

Medical Exemption Certificate .... ☐

Any gym or private club membership.............................. ☐

Store card membership .... ☐

Child(ren)'s school .... ☐

Loyalty cards (eg. Nectar, Boots Advantage, Tesco Clubcard) .... ☐

Online accounts attached to financial information or
holding card details (e.g. Paypal, iTunes) .... ☐

.... ☐

.... ☐

.... ☐

.... ☐

.... ☐

Some of these may not be relevant to you, and you may be able to think of others. As you do, make a note of them on this checklist so you can refer back to them whenever you need to.

Driving licence

If you drive or hold a provisional licence, you will need to ensure your details are up to date. The DVLA require name changes to be completed by post and to see an original marriage certificate, so this is one amendment that definitely needs to occur after you are married. The good news is that there is no charge for updating your driving licence with a change in your name.

General things to think about

In addition to the formal documentation, you will also need to consider your employers, any professional bodies you are a member of and things like email addresses. If you also have a professional public profile (i.e. as a writer or performer), you may also need to consider whether to retain your existing name (and reputation!) in this sphere of your life.

Contracts

One of the most important things to consider with regards to the legalities of your wedding is the contracts you have with your wedding suppliers. A written agreement is vitally important for several reasons, not least of which is that it gives you something to fall back on in a worst case scenario. Usually you won't need to call on this at all, but if you do you'll be glad you took the precaution! So, what should a contract with your wedding supplier contain? It will vary slightly depending on which supplier you are dealing with, but there are some essential things to always include. And remember: a truly excellent supplier will volunteer clauses themselves!

- Name of supplier, bride and groom.
- Date of wedding and broad overview of service.

- Detailed breakdown of supplier obligations, including hour-by-hour breakdown and explicit itemisation of products or services to be provided.

- Fees to be incurred for agreed services, all consultations prior to the event VAT charges where applicable, pricing structure in the event of services being required beyond agreed time.

- Deposit required/paid, balance still to be paid and agreed timeline for this.

- Policy in the event of cancellation by either party. Deadlines and penalties that will be incurred in the event of cancellation.

- Policy in the event of non-delivery and what constitutes non-delivery. For example, what sort of time delay would be unacceptable with your transport provider? Be as detailed as you can.

Remember, contracts should be drawn up with suppliers as soon as you have agreed to use them and a good supplier will have no problem with signing a written agreement with you.

Wedding insurance

Wedding insurance is an absolute must-have. Various levels are available from many insurers and should include cover for every aspect of your costs in the event of cancellation. As standard, it should provide cover for venue hire fees, cost of clothes and rings, flowers, transport, gifts, photography and videography, honeymoon, catering, cake, wedding stationery, personal accident and personal liability (i.e. damage occurring to a third party or their property as a result of your wedding.) Some providers also offer cover for counselling expenses, and if you are hiring a marquee or carrying a ceremonial sword an additional premium will have to be paid.

Also, bear in mind that insurance conditions are different for weddings that take place abroad, so make sure you read the fine print carefully, and are covered for everything you need!

Summing Up

▪ Give your notice to marry at least four weeks before you wish to marry.

▪ Contact your local registrar to find out exactly what documents you will need to bring with you to register.

▪ Don't forget the marriage schedule!

▪ Think carefully before changing your passport ahead of your wedding.

▪ Obtain detailed, written contracts from all suppliers.

▪ Buy wedding insurance.

Chapter Six

Entertainment

After the food (and hopefully the romance of the day itself!) the entertainment that you provide at your wedding will be something that your guests should remember. However, don't fall into the trap of thinking you have to spend a fortune on a lavish multisensory spectacle to keep your friends and family happy. Ultimately, they are all at your wedding because they want to be with you on this really important day and will probably appreciate something that allows them to feel close to you more than anything else. With that in mind, it is always best to choose wedding entertainment that will allow you to mingle with your guests.

Of course, there is also the pre-wedding entertainment to consider. This may include an engagement party, but this can be treated as you would any other celebration in your home or at a restaurant. Naturally, you can make it a more formal affair, and if that is the case then be reassured that your new wedding planning skills can easily be transferred.

Ultimately though, the main entertainment before the big day that will require specialist preparation is the stag or hen night. The good news is you will only be involved in preparing for one of these at the most. You may even not be involved in organising your own . . . although whether or not that is good news largely depends on your friends!

Stag and hen parties

Traditionally, the stag and hen parties are organised by the best man and bridesmaid/maid of honour respectively. Sometimes the bride or groom has a hand in the organisation and sometimes they are kept completely in the dark until the very last moment – even if that means having their blindfold removed at the airport!

Whether or not this is likely to happen to you depends entirely on you and your friends, but below are the key things to bear in mind when organising any stag or hen party:

If having a big night out on the town

- Although officially it is about celebrating 'the last night of freedom', you should never allow for a stag or hen party the night before your wedding. If you plan to be drinking, then you should aim to have the hen or stag night at least a week before the big day. You want to be able to enjoy and remember your wedding, and not look hungover, bruised or grazed in your wedding photos. You also don't want your guests to smell alcohol on your breath or, worst of all, find out about someone essential making an unscheduled trip to accident and emergency!

- Make sure there are at least a couple of people in your group who you know you will be able to rely on should the unexpected happen when you're out. They don't need to stay completely sober, but they need to be reasonably level-headed and rational even after a couple of drinks.

- Expect to be encouraged to party harder than usual and plan accordingly. Decide how you'll get home if you end up stranded. Put the number of a trustworthy cab into your phone before you leave and try and keep enough cash back to cover it separate from any other notes you have in your wallet. Check your phone is charged and take it with you. If you are actually likely to end up chained to railings somewhere, don't wear your most precious clothes.

Going abroad

- If you suspect or know that a weekend abroad is planned, try and get as much input into it as possible.

- If your friends are resistant to this, make sure at least that they are aware of any medication you need to have packed. Also ensure you have a current European Health Insurance Card (see the help list at the back of the book).

- If you are travelling within Europe but have a honeymoon booked in the Bahamas, consider finding out if you can travel on photo ID other than your passport. This minimises the crisis if it is stolen on your stag or hen do, and means you won't have any awkward explaining to do to your other half!

Something different

There really is no limit now to the ways in which you can celebrate your stag or hen night, and no 'right' or 'wrong' way to do it. So, whilst you may want to spend the night hitting the clubs and going wild, it's also ok to do something very different. The important thing is that it's something you're really happy about.

Happily, there are now many firms in the UK offering 'experiences'. Some can be bought as regular gifts, some were designed for corporate team-building exercises and some are specifically tailored to stag and hen nights, but any and all of them are open to you as options. Even if you don't immediately see something you feel you and your friends must do, it will probably open up a whole world of ideas for you to explore. Below are some different options that are already popular with stag and hen parties:

- Bungee jumping.
- Burlesque dancing lessons.
- Cheerleading lessons
- Clay pigeon shooting.
- Cocktail masterclass.
- Falconry experience.
- Gourmet cookery classes.
- Greyhound racing.
- Medieval banquets.
- Murder mystery evenings/weekends.
- Paintballing.
- Party buses/limos/cruises.
- Pole dancing lessons.
- Quad biking.
- Scuba-diving.
- Shark diving.

- Spy weekends.
- Wilderness survival.
- Wine tasting.
- Zorbing.

At the back of the book are links to a few companies that specialise in this sort of package to get you started. However, a quick search online will produce many more.

Evening/post-meal entertainment

Within the framework of the actual wedding, however, you will also need to think about several stages of entertainment. The first and most important of these is the evening or post-meal entertainment. It is particularly important that you get this right if you have guests who are not attending the ceremony, as this and the meal will be their sole experience of the day. In addition to this you will have to find something that is as broad ranging in appeal as possible and can include all your guests from ages eight to eighty! However, don't panic! There are always more options than you realise and by taking a few simple steps you can ensure that this runs as smoothly as everything else, with minimal supervision from yourself.

Doing it yourself

Music is often one of the first places that brides-to-be are willing to consider using a DIY option. After all, it is the work of moments to create an iPod playlist and rig it up to some speakers. Plus, you get to customise it completely and ensure that every last track is something you love.

Unfortunately though, some factors can also work against you. Everyone loves their own taste in music, but it's really hard to be objective about what's going to be the best fit for your guest list. More importantly, an iPod can't be adjusted to the pace of the evening, or read the mood of the guests. This is something that a wedding or function DJ will be skilled at, and it's also worth noting at this point that it's a skill a club DJ may not have, simply because they deal with very different crowd energies.

Professional options

One the other hand, if you hire a professional you can rest assured that they will be sensitive to the mood of your guests, and be able to adapt themselves accordingly. Plus, your guests may well feel less self-conscious dancing to a live DJ, band or singer than an empty floor with an mp3 player at the far end of it. This is especially important as it's likely there will be groups of people who do not know each other at your wedding, and they may be feeling considerably more shy than usual.

Alternatively, if you really want to make sure that your guests get up and on their feet, you could consider something more structured such as a barn dance or ceilidh. It doesn't matter if no one knows any of the steps as, invariably, ceilidh bands come prepared with a 'dance caller' who will introduce and announce the dancing, walk everyone through the steps in a group. In addition to this, the steps are repetitive, very simple and a great deal of fun! And you don't even have to stick to traditional celtic or country music – a good barn dance band will be able to accommodate all kinds of musical tastes. Just talk to them about your theme and see what options they can give you.

Intermediary entertainment

You may also want to think about intermediary entertainment if there are going to be long periods of waiting around. It's not essential, but if there is going to be a significant wait whilst you and your new spouse or wedding party are having photographs taken, or whilst you are waiting for your evening guests to arrive, it is worth considering. Ideally, entertainment at this stage will still allow guests to mingle and move around at short notice, so something like a close-up magician or caricaturist is ideal. Try and stay away from anything that will force your guests to be outside however, such as a fireworks display. It could end up being a big mistake if it rains!

Children's entertainment

Depending on your budget, the number of young guests you will have at your wedding and their ages, you may also need to think about children's entertainment. This can take the form of a hiring a specialist children's entertainer such as a clown or face-painter, or it could simply mean taking an additional room in your venue reception where kids can watch a video or play games if the speeches are likely to drag on. On the other hand, you could keep families together and still keep little minds entertained by providing on-table entertainment specifically made for children, such as that provided by www.busybags.biz (see the help list for further information). The entertainment bags are typically geared towards different age ranges, and may be available with different themes or levels of indulgence. Of course, for a budget option you could always put your own together, customise the contents to your heart's content and even decorate the package in line with your wedding's colours!

Whatever you decide you want to book, make sure you ask any potential entertainer the following questions:

Questions to ask all entertainers

- How much and when are the deposits and final payments due?

- Have you worked in this venue/at a wedding/with this size of crowd before?

- If the party is still going strong when you're due to leave, would you be willing to consider staying longer?

- If this happens, how much will it cost?

- What are the cancellation penalties and deadlines?

- Do you require a viewing of the space beforehand, i.e. with a view to setting up any specialist equipment?

- Tell us about your performing style and how you engage with your audience.

- What happens if one of you is sick on the day? Are you affiliated to an agency who can provide a replacement?

- Are you affiliated to any official bodies? (If so, make a note of them and investigate their membership requirements in your own time. Some, like The Magic Circle, have incredibly stringent entrance requirements and this is often an excellent indicator of quality and professionalism. Other bodies may simply be joined by paying an annual fee and largely exist as an online register of artists in that discipline. Be careful!)

- How much time do you require to set up, prepare and then pack up on the day?

- Can you supply any references?

Additional questions for live bands, DJs and musicians

- Can we hear a sample of your music?

- How long have you worked and performed together (if dealing with a live band)?

- Do you have complete control of the music list or can we and our guests make requests?

- How will you manage your breaks? (For example, some bands operate a rolling break system where one member leaves the stage for a fifteen minute break at a time, others leave the stage completely. If this is the case, or if you are working with a solo artist, you may want to provide a CD to play in their absence to keep everyone dancing!).

Additional questions for children's entertainers

- Can you provide an Enhanced Disclosure/CRB Check (England and Wales) or Protecting Vulnerable Groups Certificate (Scotland) dated within the last year? (If a performer can supply the relevant document and is happy to do so, it should definitely be viewed as a point in their favour. However, documentation proving that one is not on any offender registers costs money and may not be a priority for a small independent business. Furthermore, it is a highly confidential document and a freelancer is not legally obliged to share it with you if they do not wish to. Therefore, if it is not present it is not necessarily a reason to worry. On the other hand, if you are dealing with an agency, you should be given details on what checks the agency carries out and also how they follow up on client satisfaction.)

- Are you experienced with this age group and situation?

- Can you adapt your routine to the children's mood? (i.e. if they are all very energetic and excited when they arrive, they might not want to sit quietly and have their faces painted or watch balloon tying).

- Do you give out sweets or chocolate? (If so, you may be putting children with allergies at risk, so ask if they can supply little toys instead.)

- If considering a clown, are you willing to wear little or no makeup? (This is not as odd a request as it may sound – modern clowns are aware that younger children can find their face paint upsetting, and may be happy to accommodate this. Bear in mind that this will be dependent on the clown's performance style though, so have an open and honest discussion about if it will work.

- Are you a qualified first aider?

Summing Up

- Keep your stag and hen nights at least one week before your wedding.

- Be realistic about the amount of entertainment you need

- Have a face-to-face meeting with anyone you are considering – their ability to create rapport and put people at ease is key.

- Know what facilities (e.g. stage size, electrical outlets) your space offers.

- Don't forget the children!

Chapter Seven

Making Memories

Weddings are exciting and wonderful events and long after the day is over your mementos of the day will remain. However, you can't be everywhere at once and, as we all know, the human memory is far from infallible! So it's really important that you think carefully about how you want to record your wedding, as there are many options open to you.

Photography and videography

All photographers that are worth considering will be glad to give you a no-obligation discussion with them beforehand. This is because it benefits them as well as you, as it gives them a clear idea of what you want from your wedding, as well as crucial information about the venue and times etc. So don't be shy in asking or in sharing your own ideas! A good rapport with your photographer is essential if you are to get the most out of your wedding shoot, and one of the best ways to do this is sit down with them beforehand and chat about what you want from the day. Of course, you should always take this as an opportunity to view their previous work, (even if you have viewed plenty of images on their website), as this will give you an idea of how photographs are presented, what a full wedding shoot from this photographer will look like and the overall balance of different photographic styles. Overleaf are some of the key questions for you to ask a photographer, and some to ask yourself.

Questions for the photographer

- How would you describe your photography and working styles?

- Can we see previous examples of your work? (Ideally an example of the wedding packages you are considering, and if possible photographs at your chosen venue)

- Will you take the photographs, will you have an assistant or do you use subcontractors?

- If you use other people, is there an additional charge?

- Will you be available for all the times on the day?

- Do you shoot on film, digitally or both? (Bear in mind that colour digital photographs can be rendered into black and white or sepia toned afterwards.)

- Can you accommodate certain shots we'd like?

- What if the weather is awful?

- Do you ever do more than one wedding on a given day?

- Are you a member of any professional organisations?

- Are you insured? What happens if your equipment breaks or you are sick?

- If the event runs late, will there be an excess charge?

- What packages do you offer?

- Do you offer a pre-wedding shoot so we can 'get a feel' for each other, and if so is there a charge for this?

- Do you provide retouching, colour adjustment or other corrective services and, if so, is there any extra charge for this?

- When will I receive my prints and/or digital images?

- If I would like to order extra prints, how much will this cost and what is the procedure?

- Do you offer a videography service or can you recommend someone locally who might do this?

- Do you mind if other people take photographs whilst you do? (See 'Going Unplugged' on page 77).

How to prepare

It's just as vital that you are prepared for this conversation. Here are a few things you will want to consider:

- What do different types of photography (e.g. photojournalistic, contemporary, candid, traditional) actually look like?
- Do I want a photographer who will blend into the background or do I prefer more formal shots?
- How long do I want my photographer to stay? What parts of the day should he or she cover?
- What balance of group to couple shots do we want?
- Are there any 'simultaneous' events (i.e. pre-ceremony dressing in separate locations) that will necessitate two photographers?

After you have met

Once you have met your photographer, take time to reflect on the conversation you've had and discuss the following with your partner.

- Do we get a good feeling about this person? Are we satisfied that they have listened to and will respect our wishes?
- Did we like the quality and style of their work?
- Have we (or will we) meet everyone who is taking photographs on the day?

Digital sharing and website management

In this digital age, the sharing of photographs is no longer restricted to printing multiple copies of prints. In many ways this is excellent; you have the potential to share memories of your special day with an infinite number of people, and aside from the initial expenditure the cost is negligible or non-existent. However, these freer methods of sharing information open up other challenges, as detailed below.

Privacy Vs. accessibility

One of the key choices to make is how public you want your wedding photographs to be. If you are determined to keep them solely in hard copy or exclusively on your hard drive, then this is easily solved! However, most couples like the option of allowing friends and family to access the pictures in an electronic format, think carefully about your options:

- CD or memory stick – probably the closest electronic relative to a traditional set of prints, this gives you a reasonable degree of control over what prints are shown and to whom. Furthermore, a CD or flash drive with photographs of your wedding can be a lovely gift to send with the thank you letters to all of your guests. Be aware, however, that this offers no protection against photographs being downloaded and forwarded on. This may not concern you at all, but if it does, remember to factor it into your calculations.

- Password protected webpage – arguably the most secure and well-controlled option. Sites such as www.gettingmarried.co.uk offer sections within your account where photographs can be uploaded but only seen by people who are actually given permission by you to view them. Of course, you don't have to use a wedding website for this: blogs and basic free websites are also very useful for this and quite easy to set up. However, as with any information you would share online, exercise caution and remember that nothing on the Internet can be guaranteed to be completely tamper-proof.

- Social networking sites – if you would like to reach a much broader audience with your pictures, this is probably one of the easiest ways to do it. However, as some social networking sites have been known to change privacy settings without notifying users, (and those privacy settings can sometimes be tricky to navigate with complete confidence) this is probably best kept for photos that you are proud to show the entire world!

- Email – email is also worth considering if you would like to share just a few photographs or maybe one reasonably small video from your wedding.

Always remember though, that you will be taking up space in people's inboxes and possibly causing their systems to slow down the more images you send. Also, as with private web pages and social networking sites, all information online is susceptible to malicious attacks and security breaches.

Copyright and legal issues

Something many couples do not realise is that copyright of their wedding photographs will normally remain with the photographer, and that the photographer grants you a license to use the photographs for personal use. In nearly all cases, this will not impact you – you will still be able to print as many copies as you like of your wedding photographs (assuming you have bought a copy of the digital originals from the photographer) and display or share them with your friends as described previously. However, if you wish to sell your photographs in any way, (i.e. to a local newspaper) you must discuss this with your photographer. As the artist, he or she has to give permission for their work to be used in a commercial context, and has the right to be acknowledged as such.

The other side of copyright is that the photographer technically retains the right to use any photographs they take on their website or promotional literature etc. for marketing purposes. However, a reputable artist will be upfront about this and ask for permission in the event of them wishing to use any of your photographs. If they don't, bring the subject up yourself and make sure you understand and are happy with what will happen to your wedding pictures.

Photobooths

What are they?

Photobooths are becoming an increasingly popular way to commemorate your wedding, although they are usually used as an additional photographic option rather than the only one, as photobooths are, by their nature, static and limited in the type of photograph they can take. They operate in roughly the same way as any commercial passport photo machine, in that one to four people sit in a small curtained-off cubicle whilst their photograph is taken.

Why do people use them?

Usually, photobooths are used to create enhanced guestbooks, give guests a little personalised memento of the day or both. If renting a photobooth from a commercial company such as www.smile321.co.uk, www.rentabooth.co.uk or www.boothnation.com, you will usually be given the option of printing out photographs immediately to stick in the guest book, and possibly of having extra copies sent to you afterwards. Nearly all will send you the digital images afterwards to keep, and some offer the option of having your photographs uploaded to a Facebook, Bebo or other social networking site as your guests pose. As they are so relaxed and your guests can wander into them as they wish, photobooths can be a great way to get pictures of your friends and family having a good time – particularly if props are provided and the drinks have been flowing freely!

Hiring a photobooth

Photobooth packages vary in what they charge, but generally start at about £600. A quick search online will show you options available in your area, and if you would like to consider hiring one, below are the questions you should ask:

- What do your different packages include?

- Is there a separate set-up and dismantling fee?

- Do I have to pay for set-up time?

- Do you provide an attendant for the duration of the hire?

- Is there a charge for travelling to my area?

- Do you have public liability insurance?

- What happens if the machine breaks down on the day?

- When do you require a deposit and balance to be paid?

- What happens if I need to cancel?

DIY photobooths

Depending on the complexity of what you would like, it can be very possible to set up your own photobooth using software such as Sparkbooth or Photoboof, both of which are available to download online. In addition to photobooth software you will also need:

- A laptop.
- A webcam.
- A photo printer.
- Backdrop, table and chair.

There are various guides available on the Internet as to how to set up your own photobooth, and once again delegating this particular responsibility to a family member can be a great way to get them involved and add a little extra 'something' to your wedding for very little outlay.

Going 'unplugged'

What does it mean, and why do it?

Going unplugged means limiting photography to the professional(s) at your wedding, for at least part of the day. It may seem like a peculiar and even selfish request to ask your guests not to take snaps on their own equipment, but there are good reasons to do it. Firstly, and perhaps most importantly, it can be very disappointing to realise that half of your friends and family are only experiencing your wedding through an LCD screen. A wedding is a truly momentous and emotional occasion, and you and your guests will have only one chance to share that experience. Secondly, the composition of professional photographs can be seriously disturbed by people taking their own snaps, and this can be a great shame after taking so much care in selecting your professional photographer. This becomes even truer if your guests move into the aisle, stand on chairs or hold their equipment high in the air as they start filming.

Of course, if you are not using the services of a professional photographer or don't want to restrict your guests, then there is no reason to turn off their cameras and phones. As always, the key is to weigh up the options with your partner and do whatever feels right for you.

How to get your guests on board

If you do decide to 'go unplugged', it's really important not to alienate your guests or create a situation where it is easy for them to 'forget' your wishes. If it does happen though, don't be too upset – whoever is taking the photo is only doing so because they want permanent memories of you and the wonderful event you've created. Just wait for the next discreet opportunity, (or better yet, delegate to another trusted guest) and offer a friendly reminder to turn their equipment off.

However, if you follow some or all of the following steps you may well be able to avoid the situation altogether:

- Mention that you want to go unplugged on your wedding invites. (Don't forget to explain what it means!)

- Put a little reminder at the bottom of your service cards. Phrase it in a way that tells your guests it's about enjoying their company, and not denying them something, e.g.: 'We're overjoyed that you are here with us today, and respectfully request that you turn all cameras and phones off so you can fully experience our happiness'.

- Have your officiant announce it before the entrance of the bride.

DIY options

Disposable cameras

One of the most popular DIY options for weddings is leaving a disposable camera on each table. This way, your guests can take pictures of each other and then leave them on the tables to be developed. This is considerably less hassle than setting up a DIY photobooth, and depending on the size of your wedding party, the number of exposures per camera and the cost of developing the images, it can be cheaper too. It might also give you shots that a professional photographer wouldn't be concentrating on.

Friend or family member

If you know someone who is interested in photography and has a reasonable amount of skill and equipment, this can also be a fantastic opportunity for you. In an ideal world you get great quality photographs for minimal or zero cost, and they can offer their time and skills as a wedding present. However, this route is not without its pitfalls. To ensure that you make the most of this opportunity, ask your friend the same questions as you would of a professional photographer, and ask yourself if they are going to be happy staying a little bit outside of the partying, at least for a while. If you think the answer is no, that alcohol will make a difference or if the conversation you'd have with a professional would be too uncomfortable to have with a friend/family member: don't do it. Your friendship and your wedding photos are both too important to risk.

Summing Up

- Invest in the best quality photo option you can afford.

- Speak in person to everyone who will be taking photos.

- Inform yourself about photography styles before going for your first meeting.

- Ask about copyright.

- Think about security and sharing.

- If 'going unplugged' have several reminders, and back it up with the authority of your officiant.

Chapter Eight

Etiquette and Expectation Management

What is it, and why does it matter?

Etiquette is sometimes thought to be a redundant part of modern life, the rules of which are often thought of as being the preserve of foreign cultures or archaic ideas about how to dine. However, this is not the case. Broadly, it can also be thought of as showing consideration for others – something we hopefully all want to do! Unfortunately though, etiquette often becomes a contentious issue at weddings, and this is hardly surprising. Any event that is so steeped in tradition and carries such emotional weight is a prime candidate for attracting multiple (and very different!) ideas of 'how things should be done'. For many couples, these expectations of others can weigh very heavily on their minds, and all too often people make compromises they later regret. On the other hand, everyone wants to keep friends and family happy and let them know that they are a cherished part of the day. So what is the best way to manage this situation? This is where the 'expectation management' part comes in: by being clear in your own mind about your decisions and communicating them properly to your family, you can minimise the chance of any 'ruffled feathers'! It's a fine line to walk, but with a little forethought it's by no means impossible, and this chapter will show you how. We'll cover the main etiquette issues you could face, and will provide you with the essential tools and confidence you need to manage your particular set of circumstances with style and confidence.

Invitations

Invitations are traditionally sent out by the bride's family (or on their behalf), as historically they have been responsible for hosting and funding the wedding. However, as many people are marrying for the second time and costs are just as commonly met by the couple and the groom's family. This can mean that expectations can be different about the wording of an invitation, particularly amongst the older generation who may have a clear sense of being seen to do the 'right' thing. To help you with this, below are some wording options for different family circumstances.

Below is a traditional invite for a wedding hosted by the bride's (still married) parents. It follows the most formal format, and requesting 'the honour of your presence' indicates a religious ceremony.

Mr and Mrs John Pyrie

Request the honour of your presence

at the marriage of their daughter **Sophie-Anne**

to

Mr. Nathan McCreight

Saturday the Eighteenth of September
Two Thousand and Twelve
At two o'clock

St Paul's and St George's Church
Edinburgh

And afterwards at The Caledonian Hotel from half-past four until late

RSVP

Key facts about invitation wording

- For a less formal invitation, 'Request the pleasure of your company' can be used, or to indicate an informal or relaxed wedding 'cordially invite you' may be used.

- The child of the hosting parents is referred to by their first and middle names only (if applicable), unless their surname is different to their parents'.

- The person they are due to marry should be named in full with their preferred honorific i.e. Mr, Miss or Ms.

- All numbers including all dates should be spelt out in full.

- The date, the year and the time all have separate lines.

- For guests who are only invited to the reception, simply omit the ceremony details.

If the groom's family is hosting, the rules above can be applied just as well. But what if the families are sharing the cost, and both wish to be acknowledged as hosts? The below format is one answer. This also uses a less formal format:

The families of Miss Alicja Dziergas and Mr Dean O'Hare

Request the Pleasure of your Company

at their children's marriage

On Saturday Fourteenth of July 2012
at 11 o'clock

Lakeland Hall, Winchester

This can also be easily adapted if the couple themselves are hosting. Furthermore, in this circumstance, the couple may want to dispense with tradition entirely and craft an invitation with language that has particular resonance with them and/or fits in with their theme. This can work exceptionally well at more informal weddings, as it clearly sets a relaxed tone and raises a smile even before the guests arrive. For example:

With sweaty palms and open hearts

Dan and Mem

Invite you to share in a day of love and laughter
As they celebrate their journey from friendship into married life together

At 11am on October 9th 2012
The Freight House, Rochford, Essex

Couples with children

There are a couple of approaches to take if the couple getting married either have children together or from a previous relationship, and wish to acknowledge those children in the invitation. One way is to have the children mentioned as part of the family, as follows:

David Brookmyre and Jill Mackay

Together with their children Caronwyn and Gearóid,
Request the pleasure of your company
As they become husband and wife

At 3pm on Thursday 29th March 2012
The Judges Lodgings, York

Alternatively, you may wish to phrase the invitation as though the children themselves are hosting. This can also be a neat way to avoid parental jostling for prominence on the invitation! Better yet, as you are just replacing a parent's name with a child's, you can adapt the level of formality accordingly. For example:

Miss Helen Watson

Cordially invites you
To the marriage of her mother **Valerie Orlov**
To
Mr Ian Griffiths
At Four o'clock on the Sixteenth of April Two Thousand and Twelve
Soho House, Birmingham

Online invitations

Don't forget, you also have the option of sending your invitations electronically through a designated wedding hosting website, such as the ones listed at the back of the book. Some people may feel that this lacks the necessary ceremony or romance of a physical invitation, but others point to its ecological credentials and convenience for guests. It is a purely personal choice, but certainly one that is worth considering.

However, whatever you decide about the phrasing and format of your invitations, certain rules always apply:

▦ State if the invite extends to the ceremony, reception or evening party.

▦ Children's names should be included if invited. (It should also be made clear if children are not welcome.)

▦ Include menu selectors if necessary.

▦ If sending physical invitations include a pre-addressed envelope for the RSVP.

- Ensure the postage is correct on the nvite and RSVP, bearing in mind that shape as well as weight affects postage costs.

- RSPV address and a contact telephone number.

- Advise of the dress code

- Book yourself reminders at regular intervals to chase up those who have not responded.

- Keep a spreadsheet or list of respondents, and keep it up to date.

Seating plans

There is no getting round it – seating plans take time, effort and a lot of thought. The chances are people of all ages and backgrounds will be attending your wedding, and trying to fit them into a pattern may seem like a daunting and thankless task. After all, aren't people grown up enough to decide where they want to sit? Isn't it all just a bit fusty and outdated? More to the point, aren't you busy enough trying to organise everything else to bother with this sort of thing?

You can leave your guests to find their own seats if you really want to, but I would always advise against it. Here's why:

- **Efficiency.** Your guests will mill around for a lot longer before settling down for a meal if they are making decisions about where to sit. The larger your guest list, the more severe this delay becomes.

- **Unhappy families.** Unless you are having a child-free wedding, parents will want to sit with their young children. This can swiftly lead to several groups of people looking for three or four chairs together, which can be very stressful. Bear in mind parents of young children already have lots to watch out for in caring for their families, and may be feeling extra anxious about ensuring their kids behave. Don't give them the added pressure of having to find groups of untaken seats, or worse, asking other guests to get up and move.

- **Loneliness and boredom.** A table full of strangers is not condusive to conversation. It is good to mix up your guests a little, but when confronted with a full table of unknown quantities even the most gregarious guest can end up feeling socially isolated. This is especially true if people end up with guests who they appear to have nothing in common with.

- **Politics.** Whether it's sniping families or friends who haven't spoken since they fell out at college, some people are just better kept apart. Even if everyone is aware that they need to be mature and polite when faced with the person they'd rather not deal with, they will end up resenting you if they have to sit down to dinner together.

- **The positives!** A good seating plan will do much more than keep trouble at bay – it will actively improve the mood of your reception. If you take the time to ensure guests are seated with a couple of people they like and a couple of people they are likely to get on with, they will feel more comfortable, enjoy their day so much more and remember your wedding as that amazing day where they met their new friends.

Hopefully, this will have persuaded you that seating plans are worthwhile. Don't forget that when putting yours together you can also make use of some of the fantastic software available online to help you with this, listed at the back of the book. In the meantime, why not have a look at the suggestions below to get you started?

The top table

The top table is where the most important people in the wedding sit, including the couple. The traditional seating plan for a top table is shown below.

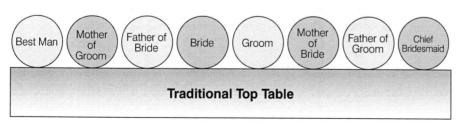

Traditional Top Table

Here is a seating plan for a top table with one remarriage (in this case the bride's parents) that keeps couples together. The best man and chief bridesmaid could still be added at each end if desired.

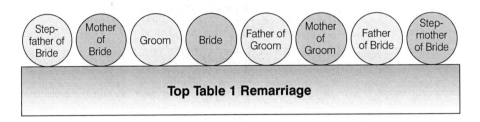

Top Table 1 Remarriage

Alternatively, both sets of parents may be remarried. This table focuses on seating married couples together, but also separate from their previous spouses.

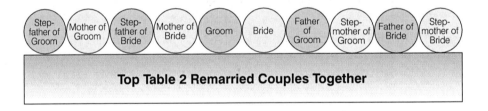

Top Table 2 Remarried Couples Together

This plan shows another table where both sets of parents have remarried, but here the priority is on the biological parents being sat at the centre of the table. However, divorced persons are still separated.

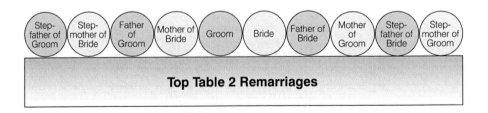

Top Table 2 Remarriages

Of course, you may feel that your top table is becoming cumbersome with 10 or 12 people, particularly if you want to keep your chief bridesmaid and best man at the end or if your overall guest list is not very large. Therefore, why not consider having two top tables? It gives each family the chance to play host, and diminishes any perceived messages about the status of a guest depending on their top table placing. This shows one way to utilise two top tables, where the focus is once again on keeping divorced parents apart.

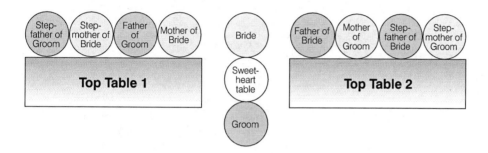

Of course, some divorcees remain on very good terms, and so seating them next to each other may not be a problem. It may well be that the bigger (or only) antagonism is between the bride and groom's families, and so this is another situation where two top tables can really save the day!

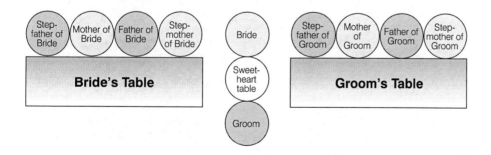

Both of these make use of the 'sweetheart table', so called because it gives you and your sweetheart some precious time alone together. However, if you are going to break up the traditional top table you may also want to consider sitting with your children, or sitting with your wedding party on a 'Friendship Table', as the two templates below show.

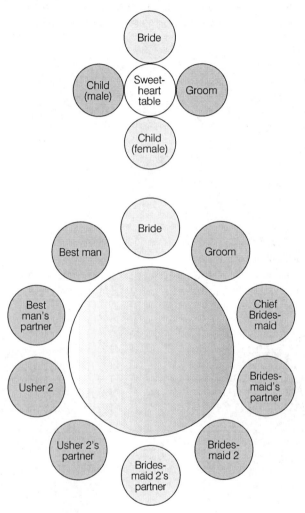

Everybody else

Now that you've sorted out the top table, you can begin to consider the rest of your list. The first things you should always consider are the practicalities: For example, do any of your guests have mobility issues, or use wheelchairs? Would anyone benefit from being particularly close to the exit or washrooms for any other reason? These guests *must* take top priority when beginning a seating plan, and you should always aim to work around them so that they are not just 'stuck on' to a table as an afterthought at the end.

Fig. 1 is the traditional table layout. People sit next to their partners, and are alternated male-female where possible. However, this is not something that must be adhered to at all costs, as fig.2 shows. After all, singles may bring friends of the same gender as a 'plus one', and you may well have guests who are in same-sex relationships.

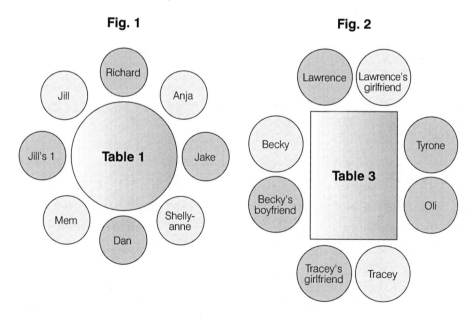

Another alternative is to have long, banqueting style tables. This can be particularly advantageous in smaller spaces, as they are very space efficient. Here, the traditional layout is to again alternate male-female-male along each side of the table, with guests sitting opposite their partners.

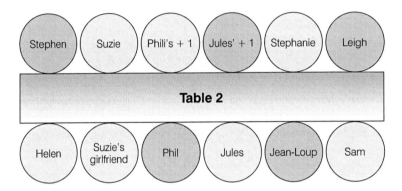

Alternatively, you could adopt the seating style preferred at some business dinners, where the seating runs male-male-female-female. This ensures everyone has at least one man and one woman to speak to over dinner, and can work equally well with banqueting or round tables, as shown below. (Note: In the banqueting table example shown, guests sit opposite their partners, and in the round table example they sit next to their partners.)

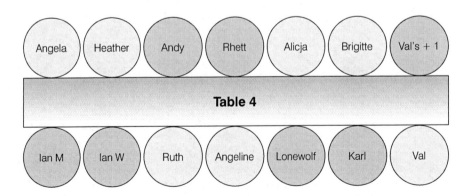

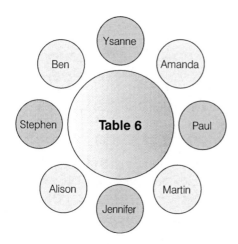

As always, the golden rule when devising a seating plan is just to and think about what will make your guests happiest.

A final thought: Unfortunately, some guests perceive their table number as a mark of their value to the couple. They may even see a seat on table nine or ten as an insult, however many times you try and explain it is just a number for the serving staff. If you think this could be an issue, why not take the opportunity to rename all your tables with something that fits in with your theme? You could use gemstones, types of flowers, the names of favourite literary characters, towns and cities that have been important to you . . . whatever takes your fancy!

Key points to remember:

▓ A seating plan will make your day run smoother.

▓ Most couples and families will value being able to sit together over one of them receiving a 'higher status' placing.

▓ Don't panic if your tables aren't perfectly symmetrical

▓ Be sensitive to people's attitudes, appearance, age, lifestyles, beliefs, behaviour and friendship histories, then group accordingly.

Gift lists

Gift lists are often a source for confusion, not least because there are so many different options available to couples getting married. However, whatever you choose as a gift list or substitute, there are several things to think carefully about. Below are the main options:

Traditional list of items

The option which is least likely to offend traditionalist guests is the list of physical items that can be purchased for your home as a couple together. Originally this was so young newly-weds would have those household essentials, but as the vast majority of couples live together before marriage and/or have bought their own possessions from years of being an independent adult, it can feel like materialism for its own sake. Ask yourself the following questions:

- Are there enough items that we really want to cover half of my guest list? This assumes you would only expect one gift from a couple, and that your single friends will be invited to bring a 'plus one'.

- Are they within the budget of people I am inviting?

- Is there a large disparity in what assorted friends and family can afford?

- How much of a price variance should I allow myself for gifts? Remember: to your guests, it can feel just as awkward with the choice between all gifts ranging from £10 and £100 as having to purchase something that is considerably above or below what they expected to pay.

- How will I share this list? Whether it is online or tied to a particular store, work out who might have difficulty viewing and purchasing items.

Money

Requesting money in one form or another in lieu of gifts is becoming increasingly common. This is partly because of the incredible costs incurred from weddings and honeymoons, house deposits etc., but also for the reasons above. Sadly though, it is also one of the more usual things to be denounced as in poor taste or even rude. So what is the best way to get around this? Ask yourself the following questions to figure out the approach that is best for you:

- Am I requesting money for a specific item e.g. a honeymoon or house deposit? Guests are often happier if they feel they are still contributing towards a gift of some description, and there are many websites that allow couples to set this up. Also, even if you are just organising your own budget-friendly weekend away, your guests will still have something to think of that they bought for you. (See thr help list for more details.)

- How should I ask guests to contribute? *Allowing people to gift as they prefer will help to make the process more comfortable, so providing several options is probably your best bet. Provide a 'letterbox' at the reception for cards, set up a website for donations and don't be surprised if some people just send a cheque in advance.*

- How and when do I tell people we'd like money? You can tell people with the invitations, or you can wait until they have accepted the invite. The former can help reduce your costs on stationery, (which always takes more budget than people expect it to!) but the latter can look less demanding. Ultimately it is a personal choice, but with the right wording either can be just fine. For example, you might try the following:

'We really hope that you will be able to share our special day, and if you would like to make a contribution to our new life together we would be most grateful for help towards .... Thank you so much!'

The key is to keep it short, phrase it as a suggestion and end with a 'thank you'. Do not, whatever you do, put your bank account details on the RSVPs or chase people for their contribution. These are both very likely to annoy your guests before they even arrive.

Charity gifts

If you're still feeling uncomfortable, why ask your guests for anything at all? One option that is becoming increasingly popular is asking guests to make a donation to charity instead of giving gifts or money. It could also give your guests less anxiety over whether they are giving you enough; with a charity, everyone knows that every bit helps.

Presents 'in kind'

As mentioned in chapter 7, presents 'in kind' can be a very attractive option for the budget-conscious bride and groom. If you know someone has suitable skills with a camera, in baking, in floristry or even tailoring, you can save yourself a significant amount of money and have the pleasure of making those friends and family feel really involved. This should always be approached with caution however, as you will be asking the person involved to make a significant commitment in terms of time and energy, and putting them under a considerable amount of pressure to get things right. If you are considering this route, sit down with the person concerned and ask them how they feel about this, and how you will both deal with it if things go wrong. Then leave them time to think about it before extracting an answer. It may seem drawn out and overcautious, but it will pay off in the long run!

'Presence, not presents'

Perhaps the easiest way to resolve a gift list quandary is to not have one at all! Weddings can also be expensive affairs for guests if they have to travel and pay for accommodation as well as buy new clothes; and being asked to pay for a gift on top of that may feel like a strain, or worse yet put people off attending. Add to this the issues of widely disparate incomes amongst the guests and a couple that have most of the things they already need, and you have three excellent reasons to drop the wedding list.

However, if you do want to take this option, be very clear about it from the offset – there's no point in leaving your guests wondering if there's nothing to wonder about! Why not use your invitations to say something like:

'We already have all the things that we need, and so all we ask is that you come and share our big day. It's your presence, not your presents that we cherish.'

Finally, there's nothing to say you can't combine two or more of these ideas! Flexibility is an excellent way of demonstrating good etiquette, but if you are sending out different messages about presents, make sure you are happy for all your guests to potentially find out.

Requesting a dress code

Oddly enough, this is one place where stipulating rules can be the kindest thing to do. It doesn't need to sound intimidating, and clarifying what you expect from your guests will be a relief to many. What is the actual definition of 'formal', after all? Or worse, 'smart-casual'? You probably have a clear idea in your own mind what both look like, but so does everyone else and it is unlikely to be a perfect match. Instead, you can opt for much clearer defined dress codes ('black tie and cocktail dress'), a more whimsical approach ('summer garden party') or explicitly link it to the event ('dress for a relaxed barbeque'). If you would also welcome your guests in regimental, clan or national dress, say so!

Obviously, if your wedding is going to be very unconventional, (i.e. you are getting married in a theme park, you want to take your wedding party ice skating or you are having a costume/theme wedding), do be upfront about this well in advance. Your guests will need as much time as possible to prepare!

Less traditional families and friend groups

Children, and multiple or missing parents

Most wedding traditions stem from a time when family units were a lot less diverse than they are now, and make the assumption that the bride and groom will have one father and one mother each, and no children. However, a family that still fits this exact model is now rarer than those that do not, so you may need to think about your options. Here are the top situations to think about:

- Walking down the aisle.
- Father-daughter and mother-son dances.
- Speeches.

Ultimately, you know your own family best and are the only one who can make key decisions about their role in the ceremony. But don't be afraid of veering away from tradition! There's nothing to say that a bride can't be walked down the aisle by her mother, child, friend or both parents, for example. An increasing number of brides are also choosing to make the journey with their fiancé, symbolising that they are already in this relationship together, or walk alone, symbolising independence and underscoring that they are entering into the marriage of their own free will.

Other ways to include people in your ceremony are to have them act as MC, or give a reading during the ceremony. But whatever you do, the key is to let everyone know that they are involved because they mean something really special to you.

Top tip:

If you want to do something unconventional, explain the reason behind your choices. When presented with the symbolism behind an act, your guests may suddenly decide your choices are beautiful and moving.

Cultural and religious considerations

Another source of conflict can be if you and your prospective partner are from different cultural or religious traditions. If this is the situation you are in, you will probably already have experience in dealing with questions from both families, and you may have questioned yourself and your values quite intently. However, as weddings are a major life event and carry huge spiritual weight in all faith traditions, the issue may well raise its head again, both in your own thoughts and from your respective communities. This also applies if one of you is an atheist, agnostic or has a belief system that whilst sincerely held, does not slot easily into one religious identity. After all, whilst it is a tempting assumption that in this scenario the partner with the acknowledged religion should be able to have the ceremony, vows and spiritual elements that are important to them and their family, it is not the case. A statement of non-belief or uncertainty is not the same as 'not caring'! Therefore, it is vitally important that you are both involved in planning this part of the day. Here are some top tips for dealing with a mixed faith marriage.

- Sit down with your partner and decide, in private, what is really important to you about the day. Try and do this as early as possible so that if you start to face pressure from outside, you'll be able to present a united front.

- Be loving, but firm, with family and friends. If you are doing something other than they expect, tell them why, but don't feel that you have to justify your decisions.

- Focus on the positives. When asked 'Why aren't you doing X?' say 'We just didn't want to/we're both making compromises *but* I am really looking forward to doing Y/having Z as part of the ceremony' etc.

A really excellent way round this could be an interfaith minister. They are able to create a ceremony with the elements that you choose, and have the flexibility to marry you anywhere. This is in contrast to a civil ceremony (which does not allow religious elements) or your existing religions (which may restrict you to marrying in a place of worship, or just not allow you to marry). Interfaith ministers are legally able to conduct weddings in Scotland and Northern Ireland, although in England and Wales a registrar will need to be present as discussed in chapter 5. For more information see the links at the end of the chapter.

Difficult family members

Unfortunately, sometimes couples are presented with someone, usually a family member, who just seems hell-bent on causing mayhem. They might be making all kinds of demands and threats about the day, and it is dreadfully wearing to have to deal with such an individual. However, if this is happening to you, rest assured that you are not alone. You are also not powerless to deal with the situation. Below are tried and tested methods of diffusing such a situation with your happiness and sanity intact!

- If you definitely know that something will be a major flashpoint, (e.g. your divorced parents have not spoken to each other civilly for over ten years, your sister thinks your maid of honour 'stole' her boyfriend, your grandmother is 'heartbroken' that you will not have a religious wedding) initiate the conversation with the person(s) concerned yourself.

- Ask them to tell you why they are upset, and if they appear to have finished talking, prompt them at least twice more to continue, even if you know what will be said. This will demonstrate a sincere interest in their viewpoint, and is an important first step in rebuilding bridges.

- If the anxiety or unhappiness is focused around a person, ask how you can help make the day easier for them. If they say 'don't let X come,' push them past that and ask what else you can do. Force them to make positive suggestions. It might be something as simple as promising they won't be on the same table.

- If the anxiety is about status, (i.e. other people passing judgement on the caterer you have used, the number of guests, the lack of religion) be polite, but calmly remind them this day is about one thing and one thing only, i.e. you and your fiancé(e) making a commitment to each other. Immediately follow this up with an inclusive statement, such as: 'now, obviously you and I know that, so does it really matter if X thinks otherwise?' It doesn't matter if there is any third party passing judgement – the important thing is that you've pulled the other person into a position of assumed wisdom and accord with you.

- If things look like they could get really grim, have someone you trust ready to step in and physically remove you from any conflict on the day. You could agree a code word in advance, although your friend may well know you well enough to spot what's going on without this. Whatever happens though, you must not be expected to referee on your wedding day. If anyone is childish enough to fight in front of you, you must walk away.

Ultimately, most families want to play nicely at a wedding. Most people want to be seen to be responsible and considerate, and this is probably because they love you . . . whether they know how to express that appropriately or not! Therefore, by following the simple steps outlined above, you should easily be able to diffuse most situations before they escalate. And even if you can't, you will definitely be able to rest in the knowledge that you have done your absolute best.

Summing Up

▓ Whatever you decide about your wedding list and dress code, communicate it clearly to your guests

▓ Focus on the positives, and think about what traditions and people you can include, rather than what you have to ignore

▓ Acknowledge any major causes for concern that people have, then thank them for being part of the day anyway.

▓ Take regular opportunities to let off steam in a safe environment!

Chapter Nine

Looking Your Best

Looking your best on your wedding day is probably going to be at the forefront of your mind, whatever the scale and formality of what you are planning. This is only to be expected, but it is very important that it doesn't become merely another source of stress for you. To avoid this, make yourself familiar with the help and advice in this chapter. That way you can be certain of feeling confident and calm with how you and your wedding party look.

For the bride

Whether you are planning on donning a traditionally extravagant white gown or something more low-key, there's no denying that the bride's appearance will be a key focus point of the day. The good news though, is that these days you can marry wearing pretty much anything you like, and there are lots of options available to you regardless of budget. Below we'll look at some of the main ones.

Boutique

A traditional wedding boutique provides many more services than offering a rail of dresses to look at. You will be given plenty of time to consider your options in comfort with any friends and family you have brought with you, and may even have exclusive use of the shop. You will also be able to draw on the knowledge and experience of the sales assistant, who will be able to offer practical advice and information about any dresses you are considering, as well as recommend accessories. Normally you will view and try on sample dresses, and when you have found the one you wish to purchase a new edition of it will be created especially for you. You will also have a series of fittings to ensure the dress fits you perfectly on the day.

Of course, this service does not come cheaply. Buying a dress through a bridal boutique will provide you with an unparalleled level of service, but it is also one of the most expensive ways to find a gown.

High street

If you are looking for something that you could wear again, or are just not interested in the classic wedding dress 'look', you could consider some of the options open to you from your local high street. This gives you an almost unlimited selection of clothes, and any level of formality you could ask for. If you are willing to consider a colour palette outside of the traditional whites and creams, your choice will increase even further. Best of all, good department stores will usually offer the services of a personal shopper, who will even be able to offer some of the qualities you would expect in a boutique. Specifically, they will listen to your wants and needs, assess your situation and budget and use their knowledge of the store's lines to provide you with your options.

Pre-loved dresses

Giving a new lease of life to an already worn wedding dress is not just cost-effective, it's also perfect for any bride who is trying to minimise the environmental impact of her wedding. After all, everything that is newly produced consumes natural resources through its composition, manufacturing process and transportation, and wedding dresses are no exception! This is why wearing a pre-loved dress is fabulous for your conscience as well as your bank balance.

There are several options available to you if you would like to explore this further, and they are as follows:

Ex-sample stock from bridal boutiques

Technically not second hand, they are not allowed to be classed as new stock if they have been used to try on or even dress mannequins in the shop. As such, they are often sold at a considerable discount on their label price.

Charity shop networks

The chances of walking into your local charity shop and simply finding the dress that you adore and that fits you perfectly is slim. However, charity shops are very aware of this and so now services such as Oxfam Bridal (www.oxfam.org.uk/wedding) exist. Oxfam list all the wedding dresses that are donated to them on the site with high quality images and clear descriptions of the status of the dress, and all of them can be bought securely online and delivered. Similarly, Barnardo's www.bridesbyappointment.co.uk operate in a similar fashion, although at the time of writing, the majority of their stock has to be viewed by visiting one of their two designated boutiques in London and Wellington.

Vintage emporiums

If you are lucky enough to live close to a clothing store that specialises in designer clothing from years gone by, this can be another potentially fruitful outlet in your search.

Online forums, auctions and local listings

Some specialist sites such as www.confetti.co.uk have forum threads specifically dedicated to the sale and exchange of second-hand wedding dresses. Similarly, local listing services such as www.gumtree.com and www.eggdrop.org are often worth checking. Finally, of course, there is always eBay (www.ebay.co.uk). However, do exercise more caution here. More so than other online channels, auction sites are particularly targeted by unscrupulous vendors selling imitation designer goods. These, of course, will probably be shoddily made as well as illegal. Unfortunately however, counterfeit wedding dresses have flooded the market in recent years, so treat this purchase with the same level-headedness that you would any online transaction. If it looks too good to be true, it probably is.

Private dressmaker

If you have a particular template or style of dress that you would like to wear but can't find an example of it to purchase directly, you may also wish to opt for the services of an individual dressmaker. Depending on the skill of the

Top tip:

If you are buying online – and therefore alone – don't be tempted to buy a dress that you will 'diet into'. It piles ridiculous pressure on you, and if you don't manage it you may be heartbroken.

dressmaker this can allow you a great deal of flexibility with regards to the design, and may even save you money. In addition to giving a custom-fit service and unique design, a good dressmaker will also be able to advise you on the suitability of certain fabrics for certain jobs, and – if you want to – advise on ways of incorporating elements of your gown into that of the bridesmaids' gowns.

The cost of having a custom-made dress or dresses, therefore varies widely. This means that you should also have a written contract with your dressmaker, and it should include the following information:

- How many fittings are to be included.
- When a toile (mock-up of the dress) will be ready
- Who will be responsible for creating each part of the dress.
- When the dress will be ready by.
- What deposit is required and when the balance will be due.
- What will happen in the event of you not liking it.

As with a wedding cake, the dress represents a considerable amount of work for your supplier, and is something that becomes more and more difficult to fix the more time passes. Therefore, it is vital that you have several fittings after your initial discussion and signing of contract and that you speak up as soon as you have any doubts!

Finally, if utilising the services of a professional dressmaker, don't be tempted to take a photograph of a designer wedding dress and ask them to duplicate it. This is an infringement of copyright, so you're essentially asking someone to break the law and put their professional name to it. What is acceptable however is taking photographs and asking for 'that shape of sleeve' or 'that style of embroidery.'

Finally, if you would prefer to hire rather than buy your wedding dress, there are firms that specialise in this. However, always check the fine print of a contract as it may be that you are expected to have the dress dry cleaned before returning it, and as dry cleaners often charge a premium for cleaning it could prove to be a false economy.

For the groom

Fairly or not, it is often much easier and cheaper to source the groom's attire for his wedding day. In fact, the biggest decision he is likely to face is whether to rent or buy his suit. There are advantages to both, as outlined below:

Advantages of hiring

- The initial outlay is less.
- Makes sense if not attending many more events where a suit (or suit of this formality) would be appropriate.

Advantages of buying

- If worn over time it becomes very cost-effective.
- It can be amended or even fully tailored to the individual, giving a much better cut.
- Bought suits are less likely to look cheap or outdated.

Bridesmaids and ushers

Difficult though it may seem at first, choosing your wedding dress is sometimes easier than co-ordinating bridesmaids' dresses and suits for your groomsmen. After all, you are now shopping for multiple people instead of one, all of whom you probably want to co-ordinate in some way but who are likely to have different body shapes. Then there is the issue of 'who pays?' The more co-ordination you require the more expensive this part of the wedding will be. Therefore, even if you only have two or three bridesmaids and groomsmen, the bill for this part of your wedding can suddenly spiral out of control.

Top tip:

Wedding magazines are a great source of inspiration for different looks. Spend some time with them and take them as a starting point to your dressmaker.

Of course, you can always ask the wedding party to pay for their own attire, but this can be a risky strategy. Not only do you run the risk of slightly wrong items being bought or just not being bought at all, but you may cause resentment. This will be particularly pronounced the more expensive garments are, and the less likely people feel they will be able to wear them again.

Top tip:

If you are making use of a shoe dyeing service such as Barbaran (www.barbaran. co.uk) or Elegant Steps (www. elegantsteps. co.uk), make sure you order all of them together as they may differ slightly in tone if they are not coloured in the same batch.

As always, there is no right or wrong answer to this conundrum – the trick is just to work out what the best option for your situation is. To help you, here are some helpful pointers for various scenarios.

Have everything (or nearly everything) co-ordinated

- Check you can afford it. Add up the cost of all items of clothing that you want to match, and multiply it by the number of people wearing it. Don't forget to include postage rates or larger size surcharges where applicable. Also include charges for bouquets and boutonnieres.

- Send people the details of what you require them to buy as soon as possible. This applies whether you are buying or not.

- Send full details. This includes the name of the item, code, price and shop details, and photographs where possible.

- Follow up. About a month after sending the information, follow up to see who has bought their clothes. Repeat at monthly intervals until everyone has their clothes.

Co-ordinating with colour

- Stipulate in detail. For example, 'anything in blue' might mean one groomsmen in a navy suit, two with different shades of blue tie and one with a duck egg shirt, when what you really hoped for was blue waistcoats.

If you are having anything custom-made locally for the wedding party, ensure you leave plenty of time for fittings. Check your master timeline for further advice.

Co-ordinating with accessories

Perhaps one of the most cost-effective ways to co-ordinate your wedding party is through accessories. For example, a particularly dramatic (but easy to achieve) effect would be to have the bridesmaids all in black dresses that they already own, but wearing identical coloured necklaces, hairpieces, shawls or gloves. These of course could be bought from any high street retailer, and deliver a very modern look with minimal effort and outlay.

Shoes and accessories

Accessories

Accessories often provide the finishing touches to your wedding party's look, and don't need to cost the earth. You can certainly ask your florist to provide little bouquets for the bridesmaids and boutonnieres for your groomsmen, but there are alternatives if you are willing to go for a less traditional look. Tutorials are abound online demonstrating techniques to make 'flowers' out of beads, ribbons or paper, or you could purchase dried or artificial flower displays intended for the home and divide them up. And of course, if using artificial flowers you can always spray them yourself to match your theme.

Shoes

Shoes, as any woman will tell you, are an essential part of finishing every look. This is never truer than on your wedding day, but you should exercise caution: it may seem only right and proper to treat yourself to that exquisite pair of designer heels that you have had your heart set on, but you will be on your feet a lot for the whole day. However, if you are adamant about stalking down the aisle in killer spikes, it is a good idea to have a pair of flip-flops or ballet pumps to change into later on. Ask someone you trust to stash them in a handbag until they are needed, and you'll be very glad you did! Your guests, meanwhile, won't notice a thing.

Hair and make-up

Getting your hair and makeup right on your big day is essential. Not only will it make you look good, it will give you the confidence you need to really shine in front of your guests. Therefore, it's really important to have the right hair and make-up artists for your big day. Here's how to get the best out of both:

- Know what you want. Are you looking for something natural? Elegant? Dramatic? Take pictures with you of the kind of look you'd like to aim for.

- Check any prospective hair and make-up artist can work from where you will be dressing on the day.

- Check the location where you will be dressing has good lighting, mirrors, electrical outlets and shower facilities

- Ask how they manage 'event' hair/make-up. You should always be offered a full trial run, and given a guarantee that full notes will be taken during this initial consultation so the artist can reproduce your look on the big day.

- If you are wearing a veil or hair accessories, take them with you. If you feel it is necessary, you may also wish to take your wedding day jewellery.

Summing Up

- Don't be afraid of stepping away from tradition if you want to.

- Don't be afraid to chase the wedding party until they all have their clothes.

- Use bridal magazines and websites for inspiration with your gown, hair and make-up as well as clothes for the wedding party.

- Arrange regular fittings wherever possible.

- Measure and order clothes for children later than the adults to try and minimise the chance of a last minute growth spurt!

Chapter Ten

On the Day

Your wedding rehearsal

Why do it and how?

Although not actually a part of the day itself, a wedding rehearsal is the most comprehensive glimpse of the day you will get before it actually happens, yet is an often overlooked part of planning. However, everyone confident of their roles and positions during the ceremony is a great advantage on the actual day, and will be especially beneficial if you have very young flower girls or pageboys. If you are having a wedding rehearsal, book it approximately two weeks before the date. This is long enough to organise a later 'emergency' rehearsal should this one fall through, but close enough to your wedding that people won't have forgotten what to do!

What should happen?

If at all possible, arrange to have your wedding rehearsal in the ceremony venue itself. This will give you the most realistic impression of the day, as well as giving you clear ideas about for how long and at roughly what speed you have to walk at, how the processional and recessional music will sound and how and where everyone should stand or sit. It's also an ideal time for any speakers to practise their readings, whilst others time them and listen from different places in the room.

Here are some other ideas for getting the most out of your wedding rehearsal:

- Practise things in the order you will do them. It will increase the sense of realism and help with the flow of events on the day.

- Don't waste time 'rehearsing' parts that don't warrant it. For example, marriage vows may not need to be rehearsed if the couple are not committing anything to memory. (Although if they are, they may still prefer to practise this in private.)

- Practise putting the rings on each other if you're not superstitious; it's always more difficult than it looks!

- Book enough time to do more than a 'quick once through'. It's likely that someone will need to start something again, and as the whole idea of a rehearsal is that people become comfortable with their roles you should allow plenty of time.

- Practise the processional and recessional to the music you will actually use, with the musician or equipment you will actually use.

- If one of your wedding party can't make it to the rehearsal, try and have someone else physically stand in for them for everyone else's sake.

- Bear in mind that you may have your photographer moving around during the ceremony. It's up to them to find good places to shoot so don't worry about it on the day, but do bear them in mind when you're working out positions for groomsmen and bridesmaids.

- Be extra patient with children, and try to give them that couple of extra moments to figure out what they're doing. It may be really tempting to prompt them, but you have a much better chance of them behaving well on the day if they are confident about what they are doing.

- Take your friends for a drink. Rehearsing anything can be a bit of a chore, so take the opportunity to say thank you and give everyone a well-earned break from the preparations.

Top tip:

If you are involving very young children, consider having one or both of their parents as nearby as possible at all times as a reassurance – after all, there's nothing to say mum can't be a bridesmaid too!

Time to get married

So, the big day is finally here. You've researched, planned and negotiated, and will already have saved yourself a great deal of heartache through judicious preparation. Well done! Stop for a minute to think about all you've accomplished, and congratulate yourself on your achievements. It's going to be a busy day, and you deserve a boost to get you going!

Last-minute checklist

Inevitably, there will always be some things that need to be checked on the very last minute. Hopefully you've been following your master timeline, and have ticked off your checkpoints along the way. Some things really do need to be confirmed on the morning though, and they are as follows:

▪ Weather – check the forecast for the last time, and ensure umbrellas are to hand if need be.

▪ Call the reception venue and check everything is on track.

▪ Check the transport taking you to the ceremony is okay.

▪ Check the best man (or person responsible) has the rings.

▪ Check any fresh floral arrangements such as bouquets and boutonnieres have not wilted at the edges, or torn. Remove any tatty-looking edges to leaves and petals.

This may seem like a nerve-wracking list of things to contemplate on the day you are actually getting married, and that's ok. The most important thing is to remember that it is most likely everything will be fine. The second most important thing is to know how to handle the unexpected should it occur.

Get the information

You may be tempted to call your wedding suppliers and let your tone of voice imply that there will be grave consequences if everything is not exactly as you specified. You may be tempted to avoid making those last-minute checks altogether. However, neither of these approaches is the best way forward.

Try and remember that your first priority is to get an accurate picture of what is going on, and for this people will have to want to talk to you. Be polite, be friendly, and listen to what is being said. If everything really sounds okay – great! Move on to your next phone call, or getting dressed if they're all done.

Being prepared that something may have happened

People get sick, get lost and get stuck in traffic. It might sound obvious, but take a moment to digest it . . . and realise it is probably not the end of the world. Let the supplier explain what is happening, thank them for their honesty and ask what will now happen. 99 times out of 100 it will mean a delay. If this is the news you're getting, ask how badly times will be affected, and remind them that as you now have other people to notify, a realistic estimate is absolutely vital. Do not be fobbed off at this point if someone is being vague or not respecting your questions. Ask to speak to someone else if necessary.

Let other people know

If there is to be delay, a phone tree is a great way to spread the word. You tell two of your bridesmaids, they each phone two people, all four of whom phone two other people, and so on. This should only be necessary for the most serious of delays however, as guests are usually quite understanding about the bride being 15 or 20 minutes late. Additionally, have your sheet of suppliers' details so any other service providers that might be affected by the delay can be notified as soon as possible. (See the template at the back of the book.)

Finding your 'co-pilot'

Perhaps the best way of all to deal with this is have someone you trust to make these phone calls and deal with any changes for you. A parent, bridesmaid or groomsman is an ideal co-pilot, but anyone who is calm and organised is fine. Ideally, they should also be physically near you on the morning of the wedding. Not only will this allow them to consult with you as quickly and cleanly as possible, but they'll be a great morale booster too!

Getting the bride dressed

If you have chosen a formal gown for your wedding, you will need to follow certain steps when getting dressed. This is nothing to do with tradition, and everything to do with ensuring you are comfortable and your dress is as safe as possible. Here are the key things to do to ensure neither you nor your dress are damaged!

- Remember the golden sequence of events: Wash, underwear, make-up, hair, shoes, dress.

- Have someone hold your dress open as you step into it. If you really must pull it over your head, hold a cotton handkerchief over your face to prevent your make-up from smudging or marking the dress

- If you have a very full skirt and forget to put your shoes on first, sit on a stool rather than a backed chair to avoid creases, and have someone else put your shoes on for you.

- If you are wearing a veil, consider wearing it off your face until the actual ceremony. Though fine, it will affect your depth perception more than you realise, and could increase your likelihood of taking a tumble.

- Get a second and third opinion on the back of your wedding dress. Make sure no buttons are misaligned, no bead is hanging off and no threads are dangling.

Take a few steps around to check your shoes are comfortable and that nothing is digging into you or slipping. Check your dress is hanging properly, and once again, you may need to ask for help at the back if your skirts are particularly voluminous!

The emergency kit

The emergency kit is an absolute must-have for every wedding. Principally, it is for the bride and then her party, but as the celebrations kick off there is an increased chance that more and more people will want access to it! Therefore, you may wish to ask the person carrying it to be reasonably discreet about it, at least initially. It may sound harsh, but if your gown suddenly snags you won't want to have already given your last safety pin to Great Aunt Mabel.

So, what should the emergency kit contain? Below is my list of absolute essentials, as well as some other popular options. Spend some time thinking about your own situation and customise your emergency kit to your own needs. Do try and keep it to a minimum though, as ideally it should fit into someone's handbag *and* leave room for their personal belongings.

Essentials

- Painkillers.
- Plasters.
- Tampons/sanitary towels.
- Mirror.
- Baby wipes/make-up remover wipes.
- Miniature bottle of tap water.
- Nail clippers/scissors.
- Miniature sewing kit.
- Safety pins.
- Tissues.

Good to have

- Mints/chewing gum.
- Mascara and lipgloss.
- Extra pair of glasses/contacts.
- Caffeine pills.
- Indigestion sweets.

- Anti-nausea pills.
- Spare earring backs.
- Miniature bottle of Dettol/antiseptic cream
- Small amount of cash.

Many of these items double up in purpose. For example, the nail clippers will also sever stray threads on a dress, and cleansing wipes will also remove some stains from fabric if applied quickly enough. Similarly, a small bottle of water is invaluable for rinsing any cuts or grazes, removing marks and giving the bride something to sip if she has been sick or thirsty. Tissues are also invaluable.

Mascara and lipgloss can also be a great idea in the event of emotions running a bit too high, as they often can. Even the most sophisticated waterproof make-up can be destroyed with enough tearfulness and wiping, so having a little something on hand to perk yourself up with is a good idea. It won't replace a professionally-applied look, but it will make any bride feel more confident about facing her friends and family again if things have seemed a bit overwhelming!

The Single Most Important Piece of Advice in This Book

Hopefully, this book has already given you lots of ideas and strategies on how to successfully plan your own wedding. However, none are more crucial than this: Enjoy your wedding. It's extremely easy for even the most organised bride to be overcome with nerves, and this is only natural. But when you are dressed and on your way to the ceremony, try to relax and just take it all in. Whatever happens, take each moment for what it is and don't fret about 'what comes next'. Most brides find that the day rushes by them in a blur anyway, so once your day is underway, just sit back, smile, and let the day happen.

Summing Up

- Have a wedding rehearsal about two weeks in advance.
- Divide duties as fairly as you can so that no one person is charged with too much responsibility.
- If the unexpected happens, don't panic.
- Put your emergency kit together a few days before.
- Relax and enjoy your day!

Chapter Eleven

After the Event

If life was fair, the end of your wedding would mean the end of planning. After all, you've worked extremely hard, and are undoubtedly looking forward to married life with your new husband or wife. Unfortunately though, there will always be one or two loose ends to tie up even after the last paper horseshoe has settled! Don't despair though – the vast bulk of your work is behind you, and, as always, you can refer to this guide to help you hit those last few targets.

Immediate priorities

There are some things that you can apply slightly more flexible deadlines to with regards to post-wedding activities. However, the following jobs do not fall into that category. They might not look big, but don't be tempted to start on anything else until you have these completed as they are important! For ease of reference they are arranged according to how much time you have between the end of your wedding and the time you must leave for your honeymoon. And remember: you can always enlist other people to help with this. Generally people will be very sympathetic to how much work you will have done already, and may even be more confident in their own ability to assist you now all the pressure is off!

24 hours or less

- Return any equipment that has been hired or rented.
- Return any family heirlooms.
- Ensure strategies for recycling are in place (see page 124).

Top tip:

Remember, if you marry on a Saturday you may need to check if your vendors will be immediately available over the weekend.

- Have clothes professionally cleaned (and stored if so desired).
- Check suitcases and travel documents are okay.

Of course, if you have less time than that before you travel, you can entrust the different steps to other people.

1 to 3 days

- All of the above.
- If any of your items are liable for damage charges (e.g. reception linens), seek clarification as soon as they are back with the vendor about any charges incurred. Of course, you should always be upfront if you know that your best friend's daughter decided to enhance the chair covers with orange crayon, but even if you think your deposit should be safe, press for a quick resolution on this.
- Check with the photographer when the proofs and prints will be ready, and make an appointment to view them.

3 days to 1 week

- All of the above.
- Check that all your suppliers have been paid.
- Follow up on any additional charges you have incurred or deposits that you need returned.

1 week to 1 month

- Call everyone who assisted in the preparation of your wedding to say thank you. You should also send them a thank you card, but as they put in a lot more effort than the regular guests make time to speak to them in person.
- Return or exchange any wedding gifts that you do not wish to keep.
- Order additional copies of the marriage certificate if necessary.
- Begin formally changing your name if applicable.

- Write and post your thank you letters.

- If you have kept any memorabilia from your wedding, ensure it is safely stored.

- Double-check bank account and credit card statements to ensure they tally with all agreed sums between yourself and any supplier.

- Distribute photographs amongst friends and family or upload onto your wedding site.

Be an ethical newly-wed

A key priority for many couples now is reducing the environmental impact of their nuptials. There are many fabulous resources that will assist you if this is a priority, and of course if you are going to do this properly you shouldn't leave it until the ceremony has happened! You may, for example, want to start with ethically mined or second-hand engagement rings, eschew all stationery (or at the very least use recycled paper and non-toxic inks for your invites) or you may seek out a clothing retailer that is committed to giving its employees a fair wage and humane working conditions. You may walk or cycle to your wedding, serve only organic, free-range or locally sourced food or refuse to use flowers that have been grown in the third world and air-freighted to Britain. Your options are literally endless, and if your conscience would prefer not to have certain elements in your wedding, then investigate the alternatives and don't worry about tradition. It is, after all, your day.

However, this paragraph deals mainly with the 'reduce, reuse, recycle' approach to being greener, as it provides a quick reminder of how to make a difference and the order in which you should approach things.

Reducing

Reducing has two main steps: firstly minimising the use of items with a short shelf life (e.g. fresh flowers), and not over-ordering anything that cannot be kept (e.g. food). However, if it is very important to you that there is an abundance of food for your guests, you can still ensure it doesn't go to waste by organising the collection and donation of all leftovers to a local homeless

Top tip:

Treat the 'thank yous' as an indulgence and not a chore. Turn the TV off, put everything else down and curl up on the couch with a drink, the list of names and the phone. You owe it to your friends to say thank you with your full attention, so enjoy the conversations guilt-free!

shelter or refuge. Get in touch with the charity you would like to donate to first, and ask if they are able to collect on a certain day at a certain time. (Or even better, take it there yourself.) Ask your venue if they can clear and store all food that is left over until the following day, or at least until your reception is over.

You could also reduce the amount of paper products you use by utilising an online RSVP service such as www.gettingmarried.co.uk , www.idealweddingwebsites.co.uk or www.myinvitationlink.com. Also, you can limit the amount of items you need to take home by hiring rather than buying table linens, napkins, chair covers and centrepieces etc., and if you do buy try to avoid disposable items such as plastic glassware.

Top tip:

It tends to be the higher end brands that are packaged in glass, and good places to start are the coffee, miniature chilled pudding, savoury dip and foreign beer sections.

Reusing

Perhaps one of the loveliest ideas is to make your ceremony and/or reception décor a part of your home, and provide daily reminder of your wedding. You could transform your escort board into a noticeboard in the kitchen, and keep any leftover favour bags or ribbons for future craft or sewing projects, for example. Alternatively, you can find some very attractive glass 'vases' at the supermarket, even if they are currently holding foodstuffs! Have a look around at what is available, and see if there are any shapes that could be a good fit with your theme. Do bear in mind, however, that once the jars are opened the contents will need to be stored or consumed. But that doesn't need to be a problem – just explain to your friends that they need to help with the wedding preparations by coming round your house and being fed, and you should have no shortage of volunteers!

Recycling

Allocate someone to collect your orders of service, menus and miscellaneous paper items for recycling. Also remember that recycling works both ways! In addition to getting the big items second hand, why not consider scouring local antique fairs and markets for quirky but distinctive centrepieces and decorations?

As with so many other aspects of your wedding, the key to being an ethical newly-wed is preparation. It is a massive topic in its own right, but the good news is that any action you take with a global conscience will have an impact.

For lots of inspiration, support and guidance, check out sites such as; www.ethicalweddings.com, www.eco-friendlyweddings.co.uk and www.greenunion.co.uk.

The honeymoon

Wherever and however you decide to honeymoon, getting it right is important. It will be a perfect opportunity to send time with your loved one and remember why you went through all the hassle of planning a wedding in the first place! The first rule of honeymooning therefore, is: make sure you have one. Even if it is just a couple of nights away in a bed & breakfast, that time together is vitally important. It may seem tempting not to bother if you are busy at work and broke after the wedding, but deciding not to bother because you can't currently afford two weeks in the Bahamas and you 'want to do it properly' is a mistake. The only way to 'do it properly' is to make sure you spend time focusing on each other.

What to look for

In some respects, what you will look for in a honeymoon will depend largely on what you as a couple want. However, there are some general tips that apply to everyone:

▓ Choose a honeymoon that you will both enjoy.

▓ Consider choosing a type of holiday that you have been on before – knowledge of what to expect might help to relax you.

▓ Go alone. No friends or family should be anywhere near you.

▓ Consider a specific all-inclusive honeymoon package if you are planning a reasonably conventional holiday. They will take a lot of the strain and stress out of planning, which is exactly what your focus should be right now.

Sending the thank you letters

If you look hard enough, you probably could find someone who will say that thank you letters are no longer required, are old-fashioned, are a waste of paper etc. However, this is not the correct attitude to take. A lot of wedding traditions and 'rules' can be adapted or cast aside according to taste, but this is one that it is best to keep. All of your friends and family will be pleased to receive them, and you should thank everyone who attended whether they bought you a present or not. Unfortunately though, thank you letters are another of those little jobs that can suddenly look a bit scary when combined with everything else, so sticking to this can test your resolve! However, it needn't. Below are the top tips for ensuring you stay on top of the pile:

Top tip:

Why not have your favourite wedding photograph made into thank you cards as a final memento for your guests?

- Get your new husband or wife to help! Ideally you can split this job 50/50, but even if you only persuade them to write a handful it will take some of the pressure off you.

- If presents arrive early, write the card early and put it to one side.

- Set yourself a target of writing five per day. Even if you have 100 guests, this will probably mean a maximum of 50 cards to send, which is only ten days' work.

- Send a physical card, and try to handwrite it no matter how bad your writing is. Your friends and family will feel much more valued if you do this rather than circulating an email or printing a standard message.

- Thank the guests, for their attendance and the specific present if they gave you one.

- Post all the cards together.

Summing Up

* Organise post-wedding plans before you get married.

* Don't be tempted to do things out of order or drop them altogether.

* Be an ethical newly-wed wherever possible, but don't be intimidated if you can't do everything.

* Choose a honeymoon that will promote ease and comfort, and give you lots of time together.

* Enjoy the start of married life!

Appendix 1

The Master Timeline

Refer to this as you are preparing for your wedding, and tick off what you've done as you go along! Don't worry if there are things in here that just don't apply to you – just ignore them or tick them off too as you prefer. You can also write in your own targets within each timeframe if need be, but don't forget to read ahead first and see if it's already on the list – it may not be as urgent as you think!

Nine-Twelve Months

Announce engagement... ☐

Calculate your budget... ☐

Make your wedding folder .... ☐

Write guest list .... ☐

Decide on approximate location, date and time of wedding.................. ☐

Interview ceremony, reception and catering suppliers .... ☐

Choose ceremony and reception location and caterer .... ☐

Set up wedding website... ☐

Decide on a broad colour scheme/theme.. ☐

Send out save the date cards.. ☐

If having a dress custom made, approach dressmakers........................ ☐

.... ☐

.... ☐

.... ☐

Six-Nine months

Select wedding party .... ☐

Decide on details of theme/colour scheme.. ☐

Choose clothes for wedding party.. ☐

Check your legal obligations and book your officiant... ☐

Interview and choose a photographer .... ☐

Interview and choose entertainers .... ☐

Revise guest list if necessary... ☐

Sign up for a gift registry if using one .... ☐

Order invitations, thank you notes and place cards .... ☐

Order wedding cake or alternative... ☐

.... ☐

.... ☐

.... ☐

Four-Six months

Book hairdresser and make-up professional.. ☐

Book honeymoon... ☐

Keep dress fitting appointments .... ☐

Book transport to and from wedding for couple and guests................................. ☐

Confirm wedding party have their clothes .... ☐

Book your florist .... ☐

Send out invitations, including menu selectors and details of gift

list and nearby accommodations if necessary .... ☐

Buy wedding rings .... ☐

.... ☐

.... ☐

.... ☐

Two-Four months

Provide caterer with all menu choices .... ☐

Order the wedding favours and decorations .... ☐

Book a rehearsal .... ☐

Write thank you cards for any presents that have arrived,

and put aside .... ☐

Check passport is valid, and if not order new one .... ☐

Draw up seating plan and if necessary, share with venue................... ☐

.... ☐

.... ☐

One-two months

Register notice to marry .... ☐

Have hair and make-up practice.. ☐

Pick up marriage schedule .... ☐

Advise caterer of any last-minute amendments .... ☐

Have final dress fitting.. ☐

.... ☐

.... ☐

Two Weeks Before

Have wedding rehearsal .... ☐

Confirm times of arrival and departure of all entertainers................... ☐

Make arrangements for the recycling or donation of any wedding

decorations or food.. ☐

Pick up dress and store it carefully .... ☐

Confirm all speakers have written their speeches .... ☐

.... ☐

.... ☐

One Week Before

Check weather forecast, obtain protection if necessary .... ☐

Recover from stag and hen night .... ☐

Hang the wedding dress up to lose any creases

.... ☐

.... ☐

.... ☐

Three Days Before

Put your emergency kit together .... ☐

Give the rings to the best man .... ☐

Check weather forecast .... ☐

.... ☐

.... ☐

.... ☐

The Night Before

Put your clothes and accessories out for morning .... ☐

Set your alarm .... ☐

Have an early night .... ☐

.... ☐

On the Morning

Make last-minute checks with suppliers .... ☐

Put this book down, and relax! .... ☐

.... ☐

Appendix 2

Questions for Potential Wedding Venues

Name of venue and contact:..

Contact number: ....Email: ....

Cost: ....

Total projected cost: £ .... + VAT @ £ .... = £ ....

Notes

Question	Y	N	Other
(If applicable) Are you legally licensed to conduct weddings?			
(If applicable) Do we need to organise the presence of a registrar?			
Do you have our preferred date free?			
Have you held a wedding ceremony/reception in here before?			
Do you require a deposit? If so, how much?			
When do you require the balance to be paid?			
What is your maximum capacity?			
Can I see photos of the venue dressed for a wedding?			
Do you have wheelchair access?			
Are any decorations included in the price? (Specify)			
Do you have someone onsite who can liaise with my suppliers?			
Can you offer a fire marshal for the day?			
Do you have a hearing aid loop system?			
Do you allow confetti?			
Do you allow photographs?			
(If appropriate) Do you include an indoor option?			
Are we allowed to bring in a caterer of our choice?			
Can we supply our own alcohol?			
Can you offer a cash bar?			
How many weeks' notice do you require for this?			
Can we decorate with our own colours and theme?			
Do you provide waiting staff?			
Will my preferred transport be able to access the premises?			
Will anybody else be present on the day, i.e. members of the public?			
What are your cancellation deadlines and penalties?			

Appendix 3

Questions for Potential Wedding Caterer

Name of caterer and contact: ....

Contact number: ....Email: ....

Price per head: ....

Total projected cost: £ .... + VAT @ £ .... = £ ....

Notes

Question	Y	N	Other
Are you available on our preferred date?			
Do you require a deposit?			
When do you require the balance to be paid?			
Have you worked at this venue before?			
Will you provide staff to serve the food?			
Can you offer my guests a choice of meals?			
(If yes) How many options per course can you offer?			
(If yes) Do you need to know guests' choices ahead of the day? How many weeks' notice is required?			
(If yes) Will this incur an additional charge? (Specify)			
Can you cater for guests with specific dietary needs? (Give details, and note any charge)			
Can you create a particular dish that we request?			
Do you provide any decoration for buffet tables?			
Do you offer children's meals?			
(If yes) What are they priced at?			
What are your cancellation deadlines and penalties?			

Appendix 4

Questions for Potential Wedding Entertainer

Name of entertainment and contact: ....

Contact number: ....Email: ....

Price per hour: ....

Total projected cost: £ .... + VAT @ £ .... = £ ....

Notes

Questions	Y	N	Other
All Entertainers			
Are you available on our preferred date?			
Do you require a deposit?			
When do you require the balance to be paid?			
Have you worked at this venue before?			
Have you worked with this size and type of audience before?			
Would you consider staying after your booked time if necessary?			
(If yes) What charges would this incur?			
Do you want to view the venue beforehand?			
Tell us about your performing style, and how you engage with the audience *(don't write here – just have a chat!)*			
Are you affiliated to an agency that can offer a replacement if you are sick on the day?			
Are you a member of any official bodies?			
How much time do you require to set up and pack up?			
Can you supply references?			
What are your cancellation deadlines and penalties?			
For Musicians			
Can we hear a sample of your music?			
How long have you performed together?			
Can our guests make requests?			
How will you manage your breaks?			
For Children's Entertainers			
Do you have a CRB/PVG/Enhanced Disclosure?			
Are you experienced with this age group and situation?			
Can you adapt your routine?			
Do you routinely give out sweets or chocolate?			
(If a clown) Is the face paint negotiable?			
Are you a qualified first aider?			

Appendix 5

Allocation of Wedding Day Duties

Allocation of duties

As discussed in chapter 2, it is by no means compulsory to assign any given task to a specific person. However, it is still a smart move to know the traditional roles fulfilled by the wedding party. This is for two reasons: firstly, it will help ensure that nothing is forgotten about, and secondly it can help guide you away from over-burdening one person with too much. As a bonus, you can also refer back to it when saying 'but it's traditional' suits your purposes!

Task	Name
Announcing each speech	
Announcing the cutting of the cake	
Announcing the entrance of the bride and groom to the reception	
Announcing the first dance	
Assisting the bride in organising wedding party dress	
Assisting the bride in wrapping table favours	
Commencing the first dance	
Cutting of the cake	
Distributing order of services	
Encouraging mingling amongst guests by initiating introductions	
Ensuring the groom gets to ceremony on time	
Ensuring the wedding presents are displayed nicely	
Ensuring the wedding presents are stored safely	
Escorting the bride's and groom's mothers to their seats	
Greeting and directing guests to their seats as they arrive	
Helping the bride dress	
Holding the bride's bouquet during the vows	
Introducing the entertainment	
Keeping rings safe until they are passed to groom/given to ring bearer	
Making the fourth and final speech, the 'Reply to the Best Man'	
Managing the bride's train as she walks down the aisle	
Marshalling people for the group photographs	
Organising bridesmaids	
Organising page boys and flower girls	
Organising stag night/hen night	
Reading out messages of goodwill from absent friends	
Second speech, after the father of the bride's	
Third speech, after the groom's	
Travelling with the bride to the ceremony	
Walking ahead of the bride up the aisle scattering petals or confetti etc.	
Walking with flower girl in recessional	
Welcoming guests to the reception	

Help List

Directory of Wedding Organisers

http://www.theweddingassociation.co.uk/

Legalities and paperwork

Direct.gov

http://www.direct.gov.uk
Government website from which copies of marriage certificates and updated passports can be ordered. Also the place to check for up-to-date marriage fees.

Citizens Advice Bureau

http://www.adviceguide.org.uk/
The Citizens Advice Bureau online guide to marriage legislation, including legal processes and timespans. Provides specific information for England, Wales, Scotland and Northern Ireland.

Home Office

www.homeoffice.gov.uk/agencies-public-bodies/crb/
Home Office website detailing the procedure and requirements to gain a clear CRB (Criminal Records Bureau) check in England and Wales.

Disclosure Scotland

www.disclosurescotland.co.uk
Website detailing the procedure and checks that individuals in Scotland need to go through to receive a clear PVG (Protecting Vulnerable Groups) check.

Insurance

https://www.ehic.org.uk
Site for ordering a European Health Insurance Card.

Compareweddinginsurance.org.uk

www.compareweddinginsurance.org.uk/
Comparison site for wedding insurance.

Interfaith organisations

The Interfaith Foundation

www.interfaithfoundation.org
Forums of support and guidance for those entering into an interfaith marriage.

The Inter-faith Marriage Network

www.interfaithmarriage.org.uk
UK-wide register of interfaith celebrants.

Children's entertainment

Event Smiles

www.eventsmiles.co.uk
Provider of entertainment boxes, including ranges for hen nights and children's wedding entertainment.

Busy Bag

www.busybags.biz
Providers of on-table wedding entertainment for children.

Stag and hen party experience providers

The Stag and Hen Experience
http://www.thestagandhenexperience.co.uk/stagweekend.asp

Experience Days
http://www.experiencedays.co.uk/

Maximise
http://www.maximise.co.uk/

Wedding suppliers

Photobooth Hire

Booth Nation
www.boothnation.com

Boothpix
www.boothpix.co.uk

Smile 321
www.smile321.co.uk

Rentapbooth
www.rentabooth.co.uk

DIY Photobooth Software

Sparkbooth
www.sparkbooth.com

Photoboof

http://photoboof.com

Pre-loved dresses

Oxfam Wedding

www.oxfam.org.uk/wedding

The charity Oxfam's online selection of second-hand wedding dresses.

Brides By Appointment

www.bridesbyappointment.co.uk

Barnardo's bridal boutique of second-hand dresses.

Confetti UK

www.confetti.co.uk

Website and online community for brides-to-be with links to suppliers, venues and online articles about all aspects of wedding planning, as well as a forum for the purchase of pre-loved dresses.

Ebay

www.ebay.co.uk

Auction site which may be used as a resource for assorted wedding paraphernalia, including wedding dresses.

Eggdrop

www.eggdropapp.com

(Currently) fee-free reverse auction application for smart phones that lists second-hand items available for sale in the local area. Available for iPhone and Android.

Gumtree

www.gumtree.com

Locally based network of sites, good for recycling or buying second-hand wedding paraphernalia.

Shoes and accessories

Elegant Steps

www.elegantsteps.co.uk
Specialist in shoe dying for brides, bridesmaids and flowergirls. Also sells a range of jewellery, tiaras, handbags and other accessories.

Barbaran

www.barbaran.co.uk
Shoe dying service.

Green weddings

Eco Friendly Weddings

www.eco-friendlyweddings.co.uk

Green Union

www.greenunion.co.uk

Ethical Weddings

www.ethicalweddings.com

Honeymoon wishlists

http://www.honeymoney.co.uk/index.asp

www.giftwrappedtravel.com

Sites offering couples the chance to build their dream honeymoon through gift list contributions.

General resources

www.weddingsday.co.uk

Website listing thousands of wedding day suppliers across the UK, as well ceremony ideas and forums.

www.confetti.co.uk

Website and online community for brides-to-be with links to suppliers, venues and online articles about all aspects of wedding planning, including a forum for the purchase of pre-loved dresses.

Wedding websites and electronic Invites

www.gettingmarried.co.uk

Allows you to custom build your own wedding site, with pages for RSVPs, menu selectors, maps and addresses of the day, a gift list, biographies of the wedding party and even a handy car-share function for guests. Photographs can also be stored after the event and are viewable with a password.

www.myinvitationlink.com

Site specialising in the creation, distribution and mapping of online save the dates, invitations and announcements.

www.idealwedding.co.uk

Allows you to custom build your own wedding site, with pages for RSVPs, menu selectors, maps and addresses of the day and a gift list.

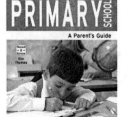
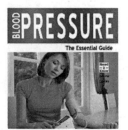
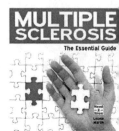